LIVING IN THE DEPOT

LIVING IN THE DEPOT

The American Land and Life Series Edited by Wayne Franklin

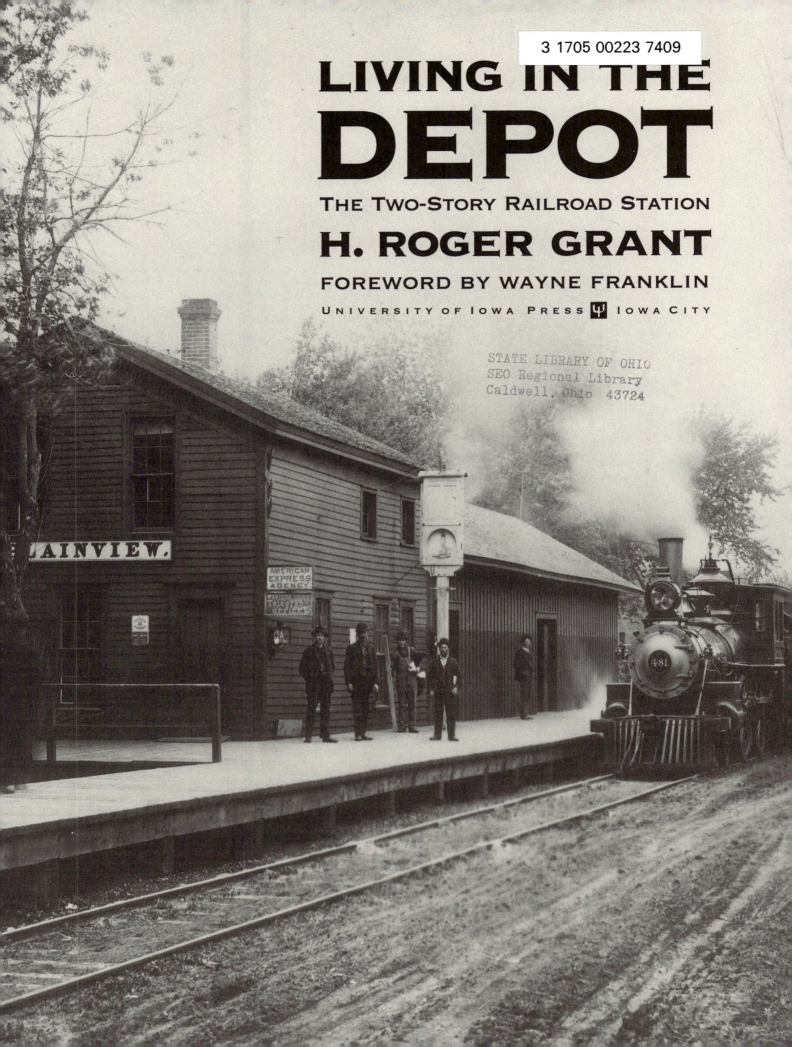

LIVING IN THE
DEPOT

THE TWO-STORY RAILROAD STATION

H. ROGER GRANT

FOREWORD BY WAYNE FRANKLIN

UNIVERSITY OF IOWA PRESS Ψ IOWA CITY

University of Iowa Press

Iowa City 52242

Copyright © 1993 by the

University of Iowa Press

All rights reserved

Printed in the United States of America

Design by Richard Hendel

Printed on acid-free paper

Library of Congress Cataloging-in-Publication Data

Grant, H. Roger, 1943–

   Living in the depot: the two-story railroad

station/by H. Roger Grant.

      p.   cm.—(American land and life series)

   Includes bibliographical references and index.

   ISBN 0-87745-403-5

   1. Railroads—United States—

Stations.   2. Railroads—Canada—

Stations.   3. Railroads—Station

work.   I. Title.   II. Series.

TF302.U54G73   1993

385′.26′097—dc20   92-37446

                                           CIP

97 96 95 94 93 C 5 4 3 2 1

FOR LOUIS W. GOODWIN & JOHN P. VANDER MAAS

CONTENTS

FOREWORD WAYNE FRANKLIN

Men in great long coats, of fur or thick wool, hurry past the end of a small depot toward the rear of a waiting train, where a small crowd has begun to gather. It is a scene that must have repeated itself over and over again in the great age of the railroads, repeated itself so often that it seems too typical to be as recalcitrantly real, as undeniably particular, as it no doubt is. The locomotive seems to have just pulled in, and something is happening right around the corner now, but the crowd has been growing so fast that it is closing like a fist over whatever it is, and the eye searches over the image but can't find the answer. It must be something important, or arousing, or urgent. Some of the people are moving so fast that they seem about to blur with their motion. They are in a hurry, but it is not clear what they are doing or what precisely has called them here, and it probably never will be. We know less about it than the young girl who stands on the end of the platform, in her fine little coat, looking vaguely in our direction, away from the crowd and whatever compels it.

With all the activity here, a modern viewer may miss one of the other hidden messages in this photo of the Illinois Central depot at Archer, Iowa, early in the twentieth century. If we let our eye wander away from the crowd, and the train, and even the little girl, and instead send it up the end wall of the unassuming depot, we will find first a ladder cutting lengthwise along the depot's wall and then, still higher up, a pair of second-story windows modestly draped with white curtains. We can bring our eye back down to the ladder later. For now, let us look at those curtains that hang so quietly behind the shut windows, pulled tight at the center as if to put a stop to the curious eye.

Curtains, of course, belong in windows, so at first everything seems as it should be, and it is only on reflection that we begin to sense how out of place these small domestic accoutrements are in a public space of such obvious activity. In fact, though, this is not just a public space. And that is exactly what the curtains are saying, exactly why they were put across the windows in the first place. The curtains inscribe a vertical boundary between the platform and the tracks and the freight room and interior depot space that occupy the first floor of the building, where so many of Archer's townspeople and visitors would ebb and flow to the tide of the Illinois Central, and the apartment on the second floor—reached, probably, by an interior staircase—where the station agent and the agent's family would live. It is hard to believe that such a family would regard this quintessentially modern space in quite the same way as the company's casual patron. It was the rare American of the railroad era who found trains unexciting, to be sure, but for families living upstairs at the depot the noisy, dirty, crowd-drawing phenomenon must have grown just a bit tedious. Perhaps that is why the young girl on the platform looks away from all the hubbub. Is she the agent's daughter? Young as she is, has all the excitement already become old hat for her?

There were other liabilities for the live-in families. Trains did not always come in the full daylight of this one photo or slow down and ease to a stop, but must often have rumbled through the dark, otherwise quiet villages of Iowa or Pennsylvania or Nova Scotia or North Carolina, shattering the peace with full-throated insistence and leaving a drifting cloud of smoke and a lingering wakefulness behind. In the process, they may have disturbed the whole village, but they woke no one with more regularity than the agent's family in its odd little house by the side of the tracks—and sometimes with a rudeness that the old spark-belching steam engines of the earlier years alone could muster. (Hence, by the way, that ladder. While it may have been used for maintenance at the depot, it also might serve as an emergency exit for a sleepy family otherwise trapped upstairs in a flaming depot. The vast majority of such structures were wood.)

To carry on with one's private life in this web of public energies must have been interesting, to say the least. Other photos in this intriguing gallery selected by well-known rail historian H. Roger Grant, primarily from the collection of John Vander Maas, catch the visual and social tensions with nice detail. There is the depot of Falls Village, Connecticut, where wash hangs drying outside while two men work on the signal. Or the view from Folsom, Pennsylvania, taken around 1920, whose details for all the world seem cozily domestic: wash strung between the posts on the little porch that nestles under a sheltering roof at the depot's end; some chairs sitting out on the porch proper, inviting a leisurely pause in the day's work; a bike and a tricycle and plants out on the lawn; even a porte cochere elegantly dressing up the far end of the building. Only the rails vaguely visible on the right betray the industrial reality of this homey scene. And that is the hallmark of many of these views, and of all the sites, whether the views capture it explicitly or not: namely, that things which one has been led to think of as occupying separate spheres in the modern landscape jostle each other relentlessly here. Work and home life, which the industrial revolution supposedly cut asunder, come together with undeniable power at this place. As an icon of the machine age that was transforming the American landscape and American social relations, the railroad impinges on these households with insistence and immediacy. There is nothing theoretical about it at all.

In Glade, West Virginia, in 1935, a woman holds a child on the second-story porch while an older child plays on the stairs and two others linger at the windows. Down on the ground beneath this family scene, however, passengers and workers occupy a very different world. In other views, white fences mark off placid gardens that abut the busy rails; milk cans wait on the platform as plastic sheeting seals the cold out from the upstairs apartment; or an agent leans on a freight wagon as two girls stand nearby on the platform and a woman peers from an open window above, its curtains flapping in the wind. One can grasp the real context for such scenes only by remembering what is temporarily not visible. Even in an odd moment of real peace like that recorded at Ericson, Nebraska, in 1903, when a man and woman and child stand on the quiet platform in what must be their best clothes, the absent train is absent only for the moment. Its potential presence conditions the whole view. Although the railroads built these live-in depots largely for practical reasons, it is hard not to take them as evocative metaphors of the modern condition. They exist at the intersection of highly charged and perhaps inevitably opposed settings—house and factory, home and road—that mark the simple oppositions of our world. Collapsing those oppositions, such oddly appealing images call into question the mental maps we make of reality and the myths by which we explain them.

Not all the views gathered here are peopled with the personae of this larger cultural drama. Most of the depots in fact stand vacant or at least temporarily deserted. Even in their style and structure, however, such otherwise quiet buildings give expression to some of the same conflicts. In recapitulating the major movements in American domestic architecture of the later nineteenth and early twentieth centuries, they join the home and the factory within their own material fabric. Older vernacular structures predating the railroad that were converted to new industrial uses most tellingly force the agrarian and industrial worlds together, since these are literal farmhouses drafted for duty in a very different reality. Many of the depots built as depots, however, employ retrospective architectural idioms that call up the same pre-industrial memories. This habit of material "quotation" was not inevitable or natural, but nonetheless it shouldn't really surprise us. Determining what style was appropriate for buildings that served the emerging industrial landscape but were located at the same time in largely agrarian small towns was problematic, after all, and the icon of the house was a plausible solution to the problem. The domestic illusion embodied in so many of these live-in depots was essentially a rhetorical ploy, rhetorical in the sense that the illusion aimed to persuade the public that the railroad did not necessarily threaten to disrupt an older order of affairs. Like gas stations early in the present century, which often aped the stylistic vocabulary of domestic architecture as if seeking to tame the wild autoscape, depot after depot assumed an architectural form that served to obscure the industrial function of the building rather than follow it.

Unlike gas stations, though, these depots were also meant to be lived in. The domestic idiom in which they were clothed, as a result, directly expressed one function even as it rhetorically disguised another. This is a matter of structural conflict as well as expressive character. Many of these rural depots look like two-story houses with long, low service wings affixed to one end, and we may at first assume that the railroad's public uses were confined largely to those wings. The space apparently set aside for domestic use seems easily read from the facade of many such depots, but the inner truth of the buildings in fact is much more slippery. In practice, as the second-story curtains in many of the buildings remind us, the first floor of the "house" itself served public purposes, and only its second floor actually was lived in. So the embedded house that seems to emerge structurally and visually from the depots as we scan them doesn't exist functionally within the building. It's part of the packaging that helped ease the "metropolitan corridor" (as John R. Stilgoe has termed the railscape) into the byways of rural North America. The "house-and-wing" in fact should be read as a large one-story industrial structure on which has been superimposed, in effect, a rooftop apartment. Unlike similar kinds of mixed structures that seem at first to bear comparison with these depots—lighthouses or tollhouses or lockkeepers' houses—the live-in depot thus used the house as icon even as it quite actually did shelter the agent and the agent's family. Structurally, a lighthouse or tollhouse is more naively a compound of a domestic unit and an industrial one, and it is usually not hard at all to see where the two units are joined. The live-in depot, however, houses people and at the same time, though not necessarily in the same space, exploits the house as a metaphor.

Maybe this is another sense in which the live-in depot helped move the nation into the modern era, for in detaching the architectural image from the accompanying structure, it pioneered a playful use of domestic imagery that continues, along the highways and commercial strips of today, to be a lively part of our material culture. If one telling feature of the commercial strip is architecture that looks like what it isn't, then it may well be that the road has merely taken over this equivocating function, too, from the railroads it has otherwise supplanted. A lot is happening in these photos, and we owe H. Roger Grant a debt of gratitude for making so much of it so engagingly available for us.

ACKNOWLEDGMENTS

This is not my first venture into writing about America's railroad stations. Charles W. Bohi and I saw Pruett Publishing Company release our collaborative study, *The Country Railroad Station in America*, in 1978, and a decade later the Center for Western Studies produced a revised and enlarged version. I have built on that body of information and that gathered for another book, *Kansas Depots*, published by the Kansas State Historical Society in 1990. And as editor of *Railroad History* since 1988, I have learned even more about transportation history, including railroad structures. That and my ongoing study of the Chicago & North Western and Erie Lackawanna railroads have broadened my knowledge about depots and the forces that created them.

Yet no book is a solo effort. I have received assistance from a variety of individuals. John Vander Maas, an enthusiastic collector of depot photographs who lives in Muscatine, Iowa, inspired this examination of the phenomenon of two-story depots with living quarters. It is his massive collection, fortunately destined for the Special Collections Department at the University of Iowa Libraries, around which this work is based. John provided me with both images and insights into depot history and lore. Louis W. Goodwin, a resident of Northfield, Connecticut, and another avid collector, likewise shared his photographs and expertise. Others who have gladly helped include Michael M. Bartles, Lincoln, Nebraska; Henry E. Bender, Jr., San Jose, California; Robert C. Brown, Plano, Texas; Keith L. Bryant, Jr., Akron, Ohio; Robert Chilcote, Bedford, Ohio; Lynn Farrar, Lafayette, California; Herbert H. Harwood, Jr., Baltimore, Maryland; Don L. Hofsommer, St. Cloud, Minnesota; Evelyn Knight, Tucson, Arizona; Arthur L. Lloyd, Portola Valley, California; Robert F. Lord, Collinsville, Connecticut; James R. McFarlane, Cape Elizabeth, Maine; Jacqueline Pryor, Sacramento, California; William F. Rapp, Crete, Nebraska; R. Dale Reeves, Whitesboro, New York; and Lloyd Reeves, Crete, Nebraska. Robert H. Jones, a retired colleague at the University of Akron, graciously and skillfully redrew the floor plans for the Columbia Southern depot at Wasco, Oregon.

I cannot omit thanking several other individuals. Robert McCown, head of Special Collections at the University of Iowa Libraries, and Wayne Franklin, professor of American

Studies and editor of the American Land and Life Series for the University of Iowa Press, provided insights and support. And I wish to acknowledge my debt to my wife, Martha Farrington Grant. This is the eleventh book that she has edited, and she remains my best critic.

INTRODUCTION

Why write a book about two-story railroad depots with living quarters? My motivations are several. As a student of American transportation history, I have been intrigued with railroads as the nation's first big business and their remarkable record for innovation prior to strict governmental regulation. My studies on the Chicago Great Western Railway and the Erie Railroad, two often-troubled carriers, reveal that they survived in part because their managers used their wits. This industry-wide push to create or modify methods to improve earnings involved construction of cost-efficient structures for local operations. Development of the combination depot was one part of this effort, as was the practical notion of housing the company's representative, the station agent, in the building. Railroad officials adapted well to their business environments, and the living-in-the-depot concept appeared widely, especially in remote places. These structures represented about one-fifth of all depots erected in the United States and Canada, with heavy concentrations in places like the Northern Plains and the Prairie Provinces. They were not rare.

Although railroads in North America continue to be of considerable economic importance, their past significance as haulers of everything from "hogs to humans" requires documentation. Admittedly, there is also a nostalgic element. In an increasingly distant past, Americans universally viewed the "deepo" as a vital community place. Whether in a vibrant metropolis or a peaceful village, train-time once meant much to residents. "The depot is always a beehive of activity," observed a midwestern businessman shortly after the turn of the century. "The hustle-bustle, which is America, can be found there." Unmistakably, the depot once served as a community's gateway to the world; with the triumph of the automobile, truck, and airplane, no single building has taken its place.

I also decided to prepare this work because of my personal interest in depots. When I was given access to John Vander Maas's premier collection of depot images, I jumped at the chance to share them with a public audience. These photographs, coupled with some from my holdings and from other sources, provide the flavor of a vanished past. They suggest the diversity and scope of architectural styling and construction found in those trackside structures that housed employees and their families. Since few of these buildings remain in railroad service and since this topic has never been examined in a book-length fashion, the living-in-the-depot project struck me as a good idea.

About the Illustrations

The railroad buff, fan, or enthusiast is ubiquitous and has been so for decades. As early as the 1840s an employee of one of America's earliest carriers, the Western Rail Road (of Massachusetts), revealed in his diary a passion for steam locomotives and the world of railroading. Organized groups of enthusiasts appeared later, likely inspired by flourishing counterparts in Great Britain. In 1921 the Railway & Locomotive Historical Society (R&LHS) began in Boston; parallel organizations also formed and expanded. Collectively, these bodies claimed thousands of active members by the 1950s, and their numbers have continued to increase. Additional railfans may not have been joiners, perhaps because they disliked organizations or because they lived in remote places. Whether unaffiliated or a member of the R&LHS, National Railway Historical Society, Railroadians of America, or some other organization, individuals who love the flanged wheel commonly share at least two characteristics: fans create their own libraries or collections of books, pamphlets, and other printed materials (for example, ephemera like timetables and name-train folders), and they take and/or collect photographs of the railroad landscape, including locomotives, rolling stock, and structures.

This hobbyist milieu produced the illustrations for this book. John Vander Maas, a longtime resident of Muscatine, Iowa, and a successful businessman, belonged to what might be called the advanced railfan category. He collected the vast majority of the following depot images. Vander Maas began to assemble his holdings during the late 1940s and initially took most photographs himself. But since he felt he was not a gifted photographer, "I fired myself from the job in 1951." He then relied on acquiring photos from more skilled shutterbugs, bought collections, and traded with others.

While railfans frequently gather depot pictures, John Vander Maas represents the most serious of station enthusiasts. He estimates that such fans total about three hundred, most of whom belong to the Railway Station Historical Society, a Crete, Nebraska-based group formed in the late 1960s. Vander Maas, who continues to pursue his hobby, deals regularly with "about fifteen serious collectors" and is probably typical. Vander Maas also resembles his collector peers in that he has a strong sense of historical purpose. "As the depots started to disappear after World War II, I wanted to preserve the past, even if that meant collecting photographs of only a name board or the former station site itself." This he did with gusto: he has gathered more than 30,000 images. The Vander Maas collection makes a major contribution to understanding the past; it allows visualization of a once-familiar form of vernacular architecture—the two-story depot with living quarters.

THE RAILROAD AND THE DEPOT

When the railroad era dawned in the United States during the 1830s, the infant industry's first years could be called its experimental phase. Companies commonly tried out a variety of practices, some of which they quickly or eventually embraced and others which they rejected in a similar fashion. While useful models existed in Europe, especially in Great Britain, American railroad promoters often wondered just how to construct and equip their properties. Unlike their counterparts in Europe, they frequently foresaw much longer railway lines but lacked easy access to enough capital to build them.

The formative years of the Erie Railroad illustrate nicely the experimental phenomenon. As the railroad era rapidly took hold, this road completed a 447-mile route from the "Ocean to the Lakes" between its founding in 1832 and 1851. Specifically, the Erie linked the New York communities of Piermont on the Hudson River, about 25 miles above New York City, and Dunkirk, on Lake Erie. When the company pushed westward through New York's rugged "Southern Tier" of counties, it built more than a hundred miles of wooden pilings upon which it planned to install track. This "railroad-on-stilts" scheme, not unknown to the contemporary railway world, seemed to offer advantages over a graded roadbed. A piled roadway "is not liable to derangement by frosts," argued an advisor; "it is not liable to be obstructed by snow; it is free from dangers of a graded road in consequence of the washing of the banks by flood and rains, and settling when set up in soft bottom, thereby requiring constant expense to adjust the road and replace the earth materials." Enthusiasts suggested, too, that "the interest on the money saved by building a pile road instead of a graded road will renew the piles, if necessary, every five years." The piling strategy failed miserably when construction difficulties dramatically increased costs; the Erie wasted about one million dollars of its meager resources on this ill-fated endeavor. By the mid-1840s railroads universally placed track directly on a graded right-of-way. While the Erie's use of pilings smacks of craziness, it seems more understandable when viewed in the context of the experimental period. It was not immediately a given that rails and ties should be installed in what became the customary fashion.[1]

Although the Erie and other pioneer railroads that employed wooden pilings quickly abandoned this practice, the matter of track gauge took much longer to decide. Indeed, some carriers never employed standard gauge (4' 8 1/2"). The Erie intentionally ignored the most popular distance between rails when it selected a width of 6 feet. Influenced by the wide-gauge (7' 1/4") Great Western Railway of England, the Erie thought that a broad width held several advantages. "These dimensions admit of wider and more commodious cars being used with safety, than can be adopted for roads of the ordinary width," explained a company official in 1841. Backers of the Erie logically concluded that larger rolling stock, with its greater overall carrying capacity, would increase operating efficiency; more cargoes meant fewer trains and employees. They also believed that an odd gauge would prevent diversion of freight shipments to connecting standard-gauge lines and thus would ensure their hold on trans-New York rail traffic. But with the integration of America's railroad network after the Civil War, the Erie and other broad-gauge roads rethought their width and accepted standard gauge by the early 1880s. This also occurred in the South. Numerous roads in Dixie for the same reason discarded "Southern gauge," which was 5 feet, and participated in a mass conversion of approximately 13,000 miles on May 31 and June 1, 1886.[2]

The major exception to this trend toward standardization of track width involved the narrow-gauge (3'0" or 3'6") craze that swept America after the Civil War. By 1885 a narrow-gauge network of 11,699 miles, or approximately 9 percent of the national railroad mileage, laced large sections of the country. Soon, though, the faulty logic of the narrow-gauge enthusiasts became evident. While these advocates ballyhooed cheap transport, they ignored the ever-present problem of incompatibility with the vast majority of America's railroad systems, which damaged their schemes. The promoters' bad judgment was partially rectified when about two-thirds of this slim-gauge track was eventually widened. By the end of the nineteenth century, then, debate over the appropriate gauge had been mostly settled.[3]

The process of determining how to create physical rights-of-way also affected the structures that emerged to serve travelers and shippers. Just as the Erie experimented with roadway and gauge, it and others did the same with depot or station structures. (Early on, "depot" came to mean the building in which a railroad conducted its business, while "station" meant this structure, other facilities—storage sheds, water tanks, and the like—and the site itself. Yet the words are often used interchangeably.) During the experimental period no railroad knew what a depot should look like, and several decades passed before company-built structures with common floor plans appeared on a regular basis.

Apparently the earliest railroad leaders did not fret much about depot design. They needed to construct their lines, provide suitable locomotives and rolling stock, and recruit reliable employees. The rail owners' goal, of course, was to start operations quickly in order to generate badly needed revenues. This was not easy because they often began with little traffic. Lacking funds, railroaders decided to use available buildings, if possible, for depot-related services.[4]

The activities of the Baltimore & Ohio Railroad (B&O) during its formative years indicate railroad officials' typical thinking about structures. Not long after the spindly little road reached Ellicotts Mills, Maryland, in May 1830, 13 miles west of its starting point on Pratt Street in Baltimore, the company decided that its passengers could use the newly completed Patapsco Hotel near its terminal point. After all, riders could fend for themselves. In fact, this had been the long-established custom for stagecoach passengers. Operators of stage lines did not usually own their station facilities; rather, private proprietors of hotels, stores, and taverns served patrons. If necessary, travelers made their own arrangements for food and lodging. Yet the infant B&O still felt the need to erect a building in Ellicotts Mills, and it constructed a type of multipurpose depot (and in the mid-1850s this structure began to serve passengers as well). The B&O wished to use its limited resources for a facility that could accommodate its shipments. The explanation is simple: merchandise—valuable less-than-carload freight—required protection from weather and thieves.[5]

Throughout the pre-Civil War period, and occasionally thereafter, railroads utilized existing buildings like the Patapsco Hotel for their station needs. Railroads, however, preferred to control these trackside structures, and they could more likely do so once their financial health improved. Failure to own them could pose problems.

Officials of the Housatonic Railroad Company, which served the Housatonic River valley in western Connecticut and later entered the New York, New Haven & Hartford system, experienced the pitfalls of a privately owned station. When surveyors located the route in the early 1840s, the hotel owner and his wife at Merwinsville (later Gaylordsville) wined and dined them at their establishment. Not surprisingly, when the Housatonic built through the area, its tracks passed next to the hotel. After the iron horse arrived, the wife became the village's first agent. But she apparently lacked the requisite skills, and her inabilities to assist in train-control work led to an accident. The railroad fired her and sent a replacement agent, and this, understandably, angered the hotel owner and his wife. When the new agent announced his presence, the proprietor asked, "Did you bring your depot with you?" The Housatonic had no choice but to build its own structure.[6]

One option that these early railroads had was to purchase properties like the hotels in Ellicotts Mills and Merwinsville and remodel them to meet their specific requirements. This phenomenon was widespread. A good example of conversion is found in Thomaston, Maine. To create what must have been one of the oldest depots ever used in the United States, the struggling 50-mile Knox & Lincoln Railroad (part of the Maine Central Railroad

The New Haven depot at Gaylordsville, Connecticut, formerly Merwinsville, adjoins the historic Merwinsville Hotel, built in 1842, which was the community's initial railroad station. Louis W. Goodwin collection.

after 1891) acquired a former cook house and servants' quarters building. This structure, built in the 1790s, was once part of Montpelier, the estate of General Henry Knox (1750–1806), an aide to George Washington during the American Revolution and the nation's first secretary of war. When the Knox & Lincoln (named for the two counties it served) pushed through the vicinity in the early 1870s, the railroad converted this two-story brick affair into a practical railroad depot. The company nailed down a wide wooden platform, necessary in part because the track lacked proper alignment with the building, added a bay window to improve visibility of the "railroad corridor," and rearranged the configuration of the first floor, including the creation of two waiting rooms. (Victorians heartily approved of separate waiting rooms for "ladies" and "gents." The "fairer sex" and children, it was thought, required protection from "coarse and vile" males.)[7]

The hotels at Ellicotts Mills and Merwinsville and the outbuilding on the former Knox estate shared an important characteristic. These structures contained upper stories that were suitable for sheltering agents and their families. While the origin of two-story depots with living quarters is unknown (a single explanation is unlikely), these preexisting edifices surely inspired railroad officials to consider such a design feature.

Perhaps carriers accidentally discovered the value of buildings which included adequate space for living. Yet such facilities appeared elsewhere and before the railway age.

M. C. R. R., Oldest building in the United States used as a R. R. Station, Thomaston, Me.

MC DEPOT THOMASTON, MAINE 1984

The former Maine Central depot, née Knox & Lincoln, at Thomastown, Maine, is seen in a 1984 photograph after its reconversion from a railroad facility to its original appearance as a cook house and servants' quarters. John P. Vander Maas collection. A picture postcard view of the Thomaston station from the early twentieth century reveals its adaptive use as a transportation property. Louis W. Goodwin collection.

Throughout Europe, in England and Switzerland particularly, two-story depots dotted the landscape. Other transport forms in America, too, provided living space for employees. This occurred along both toll roads and canals. The latter, for example, saw construction of special houses for lockkeepers and their families. While these were not public buildings, they served as integral parts of waterway operations, functioned well, and were widely known.

Surely a hallmark of American railroads during the experimental period and after was innovation. Railroad officials, who regularly showed a practical and thoughtful bent, realized that providing depots with apartments for employees and their dependents offered special dividends. The agent was essentially on duty twenty-four hours a day. "This would insure the practically continuous presence of someone to receive service and emergency messages," aptly noted the editor of a trade journal. An occupied station also meant that an agent or family member could respond quickly to any crisis, whether to call the local constabulary if a burglar entered the structure (there was widespread concern about break-ins because of cash kept in depot offices and valuable freight stored on the premises) or to report a fire to the volunteer brigade. If the railroad company carried fire-insurance protection on the structure, it could expect to receive a lower premium rate if the building was occupied.[8]

Additional advantages existed. Early on, railroad officials concluded that married agents were usually steady and reliable, and company housing attracted and kept such workers. This meshed well with the railway executives' feelings of corporate paternalism during the nineteenth and early twentieth centuries. Also, if housing was expensive or unavailable locally, an apartment pleased employees, since it was likely free or cost less than the market rate. Of course, agents would be at their place of work, making any commuting, either by foot, animal, or later bicycle or automobile, unnecessary.[9]

Other private and public businesses and groups offered housing to their employees; transportation concerns were hardly unique in doing so. America's factory owners frequently provided living accommodations for their operatives, particularly unmarried females. They did so by erecting barracks-type quarters or detached, simply designed dwellings within easy walking distance of the mills. Bearing even closer likeness to depots with upstairs living space were county jail/sheriff's residence buildings. These structures, the result of a nationwide effort to reform penal conditions after the Civil War, housed prisoners, of course, but also the county sheriff and his family in an attached apartment or wing. The jail, except for its cells, resembled the sheriff's residence; these buildings commonly sported "high-style" architecture, spacious interiors on two or three floors, and brick construction.

This public complex, especially popular in the Midwest, stood near the courthouse for practical reasons and served as a source of civic pride, not unlike how residents viewed the courthouse or even the railway station.[10]

When manufacturing concerns and public bodies provided employee housing, they never did so in exactly the same fashion. Their structures varied, although they might share some common characteristics. Similarly, railroad companies embraced different approaches. Since literally hundreds of carriers participated in the process of depot building, they had many ideas about design, including whether to provide agents' quarters. By the close of the experimental period, however, carriers had come to agree on one general type of depot. They nearly all embraced the combination structure for their smaller station locations "where the amount of freight or the volume of the passenger business does not warrant the construction of separate freight-house or a separate passenger depot." Probably 75,000 of these compact and functional structures stood at trackside by World War I and provided convenient places for railroads to offer their multiple services. Generally, these combination depots contained three track-level parts: a waiting room (or perhaps rooms), a central office, and a freight-baggage section. If the railroad opted for living space, it typically, but not always, placed it on a second floor. In this way family members would be kept away from railroad operations, and extensions to the building (usually for additional freight storage) could occur without necessitating wholesale remodeling.[11]

About the time railroads considered combination depots, including ones with apartment space, a few carriers entered, albeit briefly, the building of station hotels. As with other contemporary structures, European experiences and perceived needs inspired these projects. With rapid expansion of the railroad network by midcentury and before widespread usage of dining and sleeping cars—heralded by the 1880s as "hotels on wheels"—the need to provide travelers with more than transport by chair car seemed obvious to some roads. Thus riders could travel all day by coach and stop at these convenient station hotels (or at privately operated ones) for hot meals and comfortable overnight lodging. The Erie, the quintessential experimenter during and after the demonstration period, erected its massive Starrucca House on its mainline at Susquehanna, Pennsylvania, about 1865, and an affiliate, the Atlantic & Great Western, built the equally impressive McHenry House at Meadville, Pennsylvania. Of course, what was considered to be a logical step in the development of railroad structures quickly became obsolete, although some station hotels remained open for decades, usually under private control.[12]

The two-story depot with living space spread widely; it hardly proved to be a dead end of design. Much of the United States, excluding parts of the South, and also Canada sported occupied stations. Nearly all of these structures were built from the end of the Civil

Typical of the genre of railroad hotels built during the mid-nineteenth century was the one that served patrons of the Erie Railroad at Susquehanna, Pennsylvania. Author's collection.

War to World War II, with most before World War I, coinciding with the boom in new-line construction. Except in sections of the American Great Plains and the Canadian West, the railroad "frontier" closed during the 1910s.

The general absence of inhabited depots in the South is somewhat curious, and reasons for this can only be surmised. Likely there was never a pressing need. The iron horse arrived usually after the settlement process, and communities probably had adequate housing. Before the emergence of several vigorous regional carriers at the end of the nineteenth century, short line railroads predominated. The chronic shortage of capital, especially after the Civil War when the region became an economic backwater, meant that the South's "inability, generally speaking, to underwrite vast enterprise in any form, . . . contributed to the building of a multitude of small railroads rather than their unification in one or two comprehensive systems." These puny pikes operated their trains at slow speeds over wobbly tracks and in a simple fashion. Carriers, therefore, could employ local custodians instead of skilled employees. These individuals who lived nearby and worked for low wages usually lacked knowledge of telegraphy but mastered selling tickets, handling freight, maintaining waiting rooms (appearance of "Jim Crow" laws required separate areas for African-Americans), and performing other chores. Furthermore, the South lacked major urban centers, which negated commuter service. There was often no compelling reason, then, to have an agent on the premises around the clock.[13]

A further explanation involved costs. The weak financial condition of southern railroads meant that expenses had to be watched carefully. Erecting scores of depots with apartment space would surely increase expenditures, likely by several hundred dollars for each building. Understandably, southern roads used existing structures when practical, and these were often the ubiquitous country stores. Companies paid proprietors modest salaries or commissions for their station work, reminiscent of how impoverished early pikes managed the problem.

When railroads in the South decided to provide apartment space, they commonly did so in a meager way. For example, the 562-mile Savannah, Florida & Western Railway, a later component of the Atlantic Coast Line, used a standard combination plan during the late nineteenth century that included only a single room, approximately 15-feet square. The company failed to provide the agent with a kitchen or even additional storage space for personal possessions. A major exception to this pattern was the Chesapeake & Ohio Railway (C&O), a prosperous coal carrier which linked Newport News, Virginia, with Cincinnati, Ohio. This road, which hardly resembled others in the South, designed a combination depot in 1883 which contained a 12′ × 14′ living room and an 11′ × 14′ kitchen on the ground floor and two 14′ × 16′ bedrooms on the upper floor. The C&O called this design its "Plan A."[14]

Yet additional multiple-story, railroad-built structures appeared below the Mason-Dixon line. These buildings, however, did not provide apartments but rather offices. The larger railroads throughout the United States and Canada required considerable space at division and crew-change points and placed work areas, such as a room for train dispatchers, over typical combination-type floor plans. This type of construction was similar to that in the busiest communities, where separate freight houses included office space for freight agents, clerks, and helpers.

While sections of the South resembled New England and Middle Atlantic states in having been settled before the railroad age, striking differences existed by the Gilded Age. What might be loosely called the Northeast enjoyed dramatically greater prosperity, boasted a larger and less agrarian population, and attracted vast amounts of investment capital. Not surprisingly, these states witnessed a plethora of railroad construction. Rather than being an assortment of little roads, systems rapidly emerged, including the mighty New York Central and the Pennsylvania, the former immodestly calling itself the "Greatest Railroad in the World" and the latter the "Standard Railroad of the World."

Not every road in the Northeast embraced the two-story depot with living quarters. Scores of companies decided that the ever-popular one-story combination depot adequately met their needs. Likely they lacked either isolated stations (sufficient local housing existed) or commuter operations, common explanations why occupied depots appeared in this region. Still, some carriers that traversed lightly populated territory or offered commuter service rejected depots with living quarters. This decision was highly individualistic, probably determined by the railroad's chief engineer or other ranking officers. And these officials might change their minds.

The depot design policies of the 500-mile New York, West Shore & Buffalo Railway, or West Shore, show why it is difficult to generalize about reasons for the inclusion of living quarters. This road served remote villages in the Empire State, especially in the Catskills, and operated commuter trains between Newburgh, New York, and Weehawken, New Jersey, with ferryboat access to Manhattan. When the West Shore adopted a set of standard depot drawings in the late 1880s for its smaller stations "which are not important enough to require the preparation of separate designs," it eschewed living quarters. (And it did so for larger depots, too.) Yet several of these standard plans included a second story. This addition served largely for decoration, understandable since Victorians loved architectural ornamentation.[15]

Northeastern railroads, nonetheless, constructed occupied depots for the reason that led to their popularity in other sections of the continent, namely to provide housing in remote areas. Roads like the Adirondack & St. Lawrence; Bangor & Aroostock; Boston & Maine; Lehigh Valley; New York, Ontario & Western; Montpelier & Wells River; and St. Johnsbury & Lake Champlain erected structures to accommodate agents and their families. These companies established stations in out-of-the-way places, and they needed to respond to an acute shortage of housing.[16]

The Bangor & Aroostock's (BAR) response represents one method of dealing with the housing shortage. This company, which linked northern Maine to New England and was the approximate size of the West Shore, served some sparsely settled territories. If the BAR wanted agents at remote wood yards or railroad junctions, then live-in depots made sense. The company also liked standardized plans; they were convenient and reduced construction costs. Depots at Brownville Junction, Glenburn, North Bangor, and Winterport, all in the Pine Tree State, attest to the BAR's endorsement of carbon-copy architecture for its occupied structures.[17]

Although the Bangor & Aroostock's interest in live-in depots built to a standard plan illustrates rationality, a more hit-or-miss approach and probably one more typical of carriers of southern New England and the Middle Atlantic states is found with some stations along the New York, New Haven & Hartford Railroad, or the New Haven. A consolidation of numerous early roads in 1872, the New Haven inherited a hodgepodge of trackside structures, including ones recycled from private dwellings, hotels, and stores. Apparently the New Haven and its predecessor firms, for instance the Old Colony Railroad in Massachusetts which joined the New Haven in 1893, liked what might be dubbed the farmhouse style of architecture. These designs varied greatly and more resembled a house than what might at first glance be considered a depot. Still these structures provided living space and "were built from the ground up by these railroads and were not former anythings."[18]

Other regional railroads, particularly those that operated commuter trains, at times found it desirable to recycle an existing building which contained an upper floor appropriate for an agent's apartment or to build ones so designed. While the New Haven, a premier commuter road by the turn of the century, rejected live-in structures along its busy commuter corridor between New Haven and New York City, other area roads, for example, the Baltimore & Ohio, Erie, Long Island, Pennsylvania, and Philadelphia & Reading, did not. They and their predecessors or affiliates often used extant buildings or constructed ones to their own design along these heavily traveled arteries.[19]

If a rail carrier built a depot with living quarters in this part of the country, the structure likely sported fine building features and "modern" amenities, water and indoor plumbing. When the Lehigh Valley Railroad, a rich anthracite-carrying road with modest commuter operations between New York City and Easton, Pennsylvania, constructed a nonstandard passenger depot at Picton, New Jersey, around 1900, it did so in a grand style. The company installed stained glass in the door transoms, used ornamental siding on the exterior, and selected durable slate for the roof. Furthermore, the Lehigh Valley included an agent's apartment in this approximately 20' × 40' two-and-a-half-story frame structure. (The depot also contained modest front and rear projections, the former the agent's office and the latter a "Gents Toilet.") The second floor featured "a living-room; kitchen; three bedrooms; a bath-room; and a toilet-room." The railroad also opted for "a cellar under the building, with a cistern, coal-bin, heater, etc." Rather cozy, the Picton structure gave the live-in employee state-of-the-art accommodations, but it was not replicated elsewhere along the Black Diamond Route.[20]

Once again the occurrence of depots with agents' quarters seems almost at random. "I've not been able to correlate this with the type of community, location, period, specific railroad, or astrological influence," concluded Herbert H. Harwood, Jr., an authority on such buildings in the Middle Atlantic region. Structures in the greater Philadelphia commuter area illustrate his point. The Pennsylvania Railroad and an important predecessor, the Philadelphia, Wilmington & Baltimore, which it acquired in 1881, routinely included second-floor living space for its agents between the Civil War and the beginning of the twentieth century. Somewhat oddly, the mostly standardized brick depots constructed on the Pennsylvania's Chestnut Hill branch between 1884 and 1887 were originally single-story structures but were rebuilt by the company in 1891 as two-story ones to accommodate agents. On the other hand, the North Pennsylvania Railroad, which joined the Philadelphia & Reading (Reading) in 1879, built primarily single-story depots during its independent years. The Reading's own original structures from the pre-Civil War years were mostly two-story buildings; later in the nineteenth century the expanded road built both types.[21]

Yet a unifying concept exists. By the late nineteenth century those who operated commuter roads in Philadelphia and elsewhere believed that "their suburban stations should be more than routine engineering department products." Architecturally pleasing structures would surely satisfy patrons and be positive advertisements; after all, criticism of railroads increased dramatically during the period, and companies grew more sensitive to problems of image. They realized that "a well-designed railroad station has come to be looked upon by the people at large as an avowed asset to the small town or village seeking growth and development." So when the Reading, for example, built new depots along its sprawling network in the greater Philadelphia area, it frequently chose a "picturesque cottage" style, characterized by a pleasing assortment of angles which gave these structures a different appearance when viewed from either end. Those that contained agents' living quarters were one and a half stories and were "quite stunning."[22]

Beyond the Appalachians, in the Old Northwest, the popularity of two-story depots with living space varied more by geography than by company. The lower three of the five states that once comprised the Northwest Territory—Ohio, Indiana, and Illinois—contained few of these structures. In Ohio, for instance, they were rare, except in the state's southeastern coalfields where several roads, most notably the Hocking Valley, occasionally used inhabited general stores for their stations. And when the Baltimore & Ohio pushed a line through northern Ohio in the 1880s, it selected a standardized two-story plan with agents' quarters for Creston and Greenwich, important railroad junctions 34 miles apart. The principal exception to the one-story structure involved several carriers in greater Chicago. The Baltimore & Ohio; Chicago, Burlington & Quincy; Chicago, Rock Island & Pacific; Chicago & Western Indiana; and the Illinois Central opted for some two-story occupied depots to serve commuter stations both inside and outside the Windy City.[23]

The situation changed dramatically in the two other states of the Old Northwest, Michigan and Wisconsin. While commuter service was not the impetus, various roads perceived the need to offer housing. The Chicago & North Western; Chicago, Milwaukee & St. Paul (initially called the St. Paul and then the Milwaukee); Duluth, South Shore & Atlantic; Pere Marquette; Minneapolis, St. Paul & Sault Ste. Marie (Soo Line); and the Wisconsin

Central, long affiliated with the Soo, erected scores of two-story depots with apartments, especially in Michigan's Upper Peninsula and Wisconsin's northern region.

Architectural variations occurred. For one thing, these depots differed in their exterior styles from road to road, paralleling patterns in the East and elsewhere. Also they were less ornate as a group than those built by some eastern roads. Time of construction (late-Victorian depots tended to be less fussy architecturally than those of the 1870s and 1880s), financial considerations, and attitudes of engineering departments likely contributed to such sectional differences. The Milwaukee, for example, in 1901 chose a 60′ × 24′ combination depot, a popular overall dimension, which featured a typical upstairs floorplan: kitchen (11′ × 12′6″), sitting room (11′6″ × 12′6″), two bedrooms (13′ × 10′ and 11′ × 10′), and small pantry and hall. Three years earlier the Wisconsin Central adopted a plan for a 49′ × 17′ depot which offered a cozier second-floor layout: kitchen (22′ × 10′), living room (24′6″ × 15′), storeroom (13′ × 5′3″), and hall. The living room surely doubled as the bedroom, and perhaps the storeroom and kitchen contained a bed as well. Standardized drawings attest to the diversity of this genre.[24]

Further west, railroads in Minnesota, Iowa, and Missouri replicated the kinds of depots that were part of the station-scape of the Old Northwest. Some carriers did not utilize the two-story depot with agent's apartment plan. The Chicago, Burlington & Quincy, for one, usually saw no need to erect such structures. Although it operated more than a thousand miles of track in Iowa, it built two-story depots with living quarters only twice. One served a booming coal-mining camp, Brazil, and the other a remote branch line crossing, Merle Junction (the latter used a former farmhouse). Those roads that erected this type of depot either served territory on both sides of the Mississippi River or merely found such structures practical. Examples abound. For instance, the Milwaukee constructed its 24′ × 60′ plan in a number of communities in Iowa, Michigan, and Missouri; the Toledo & North Western, part of the Chicago & North Western system, built more than a dozen nearly identical two-story depots with apartments along its several hundred miles of main and branch lines in northern Iowa.[25]

The West became the heartland of the living-in-the-depot phenomenon, mostly in large sections of the Northern Plains, Prairie Provinces of Canada, Far West, and Southwest. Hundreds of these distinctive buildings blossomed forth between the 1870s and the 1940s. Indeed, the West is where standardized structures, including those built by railroads, became the most pronounced. The settlement of the West coincided with the triumph of standardization in national life. While average citizens, particularly rough-and-ready westerners, likely expressed an abiding belief in individualism as it allegedly sprang from the frontier experience, they quickly accepted a homogenized way of life. Standardized brand-

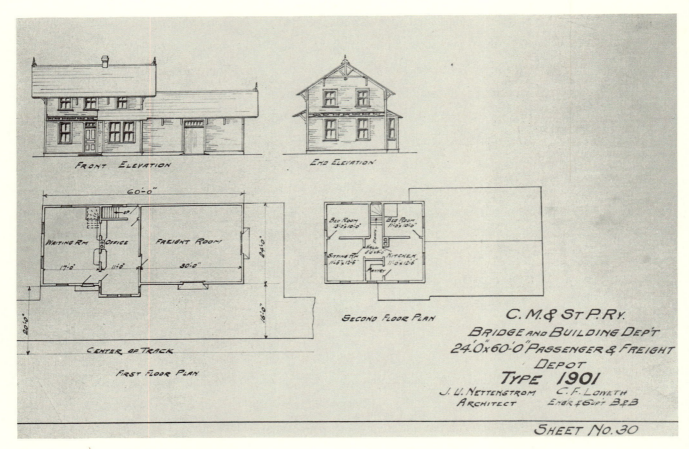

FRONT ELEVATION

END ELEVATION

60'-0"

WAITING RM | Office | FREIGHT ROOM

17'-0" | 11'-0" | 30'-0"

24'-0"

18'-0"

20'-0"

CENTER OF TRACK

FIRST FLOOR PLAN

Bed Room
13'-0"x10'-0"
Bed Room
11'-0"x10'-0"

Store Rm
11'-5"x12'-6"
Kitchen
11'-0"x12'-6"

SECOND FLOOR PLAN

C. M. & St. P. Ry.
BRIDGE AND BUILDING DEP'T
24'-0"x60'-0" PASSENGER & FREIGHT
DEPOT
TYPE 1901
J. U. NETTENSTROM
ARCHITECT
C. F. LOWETH
Engr & Supt B & B

SHEET NO. 30

The Chicago, Milwaukee & St. Paul Railway
turned to its bridge and building department in
1900 to design a 24' x 60' depot with living
quarters. These were used mostly as replacement
structures. Author's collection.

name consumer products, for instance, became common by the beginning of the twentieth century. Historian Lewis Atherton demonstrated how the "Battle of the Brands" shortly after the Civil War revolutionized the country's merchandising and buying habits. "Once Singer Sewing Machines had been widely advertized," Atherton wrote by way of illustration, "women demanded to see them before making a final choice, and retailers had to carry Singer models or lose trade to stores which did." Standardization came in diverse forms: time zones, dress patterns, and even the rules for the national pastime. And railroads, the nation's first big business, embraced standardization with enthusiasm: rolling stock (the celebrated 4-4-0 steam locomotive became known as the American Standard), couplers, signals, and much more.[26]

Standardization similarly invaded American architecture. During the latter part of the nineteenth century, decorative building parts for both internal and external use could easily be ordered from scores of millwork factories; one had only to choose from their illustrated

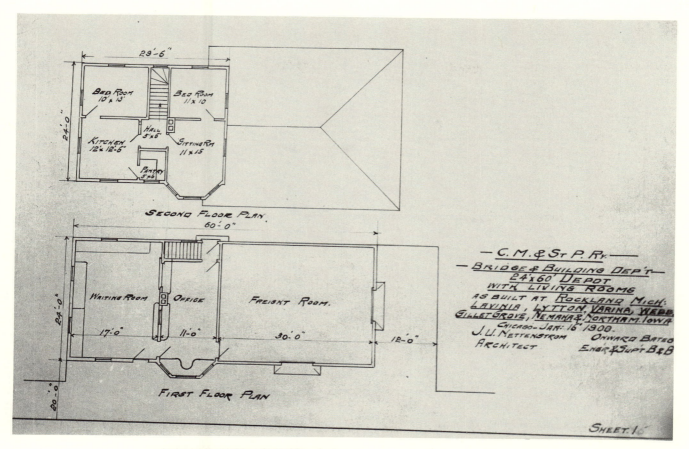

SECOND FLOOR PLAN.

FIRST FLOOR PLAN

— C. M. & St. P. Ry. —
— BRIDGE & BUILDING DEP'T —
24x60' DEPOT
WITH LIVING ROOMS
AS BUILT AT ROCKLAND MICH.
LAVINIA, LYTTON, VARINA, WEBB
GILLET GROVE, NEMAHA & NORTHAM IOWA
CHICAGO — JAN: 16 1900.
J.U. NETTENSTROM   ONWARD BATES
ARCHITECT   ENGR & SUPT B&B

SHEET. 16

At the turn of the century the Milwaukee Road's
buildings officer oversaw creation of an attractive
24' x 60' two-story depot with agent's apartment.
The one at Albert City, Iowa, on the company's
Storm Lake branch, represents this design. John P.
Vander Maas collection.

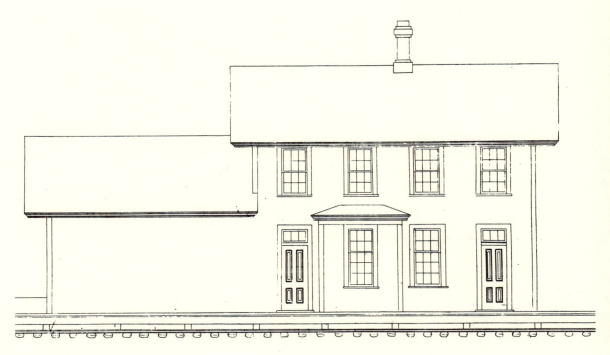

The Toledo & North Western Railway erected
spartan two-story depots built to its Standard No. 2
plan throughout large sections of Iowa late in the
nineteenth century. Author's collection.

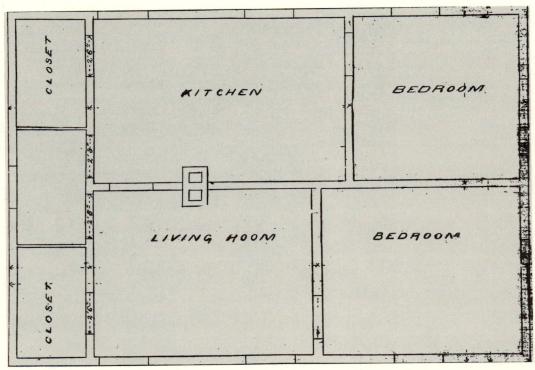

The Toledo & North Western provided an agent
with a basic apartment, as seen in this second-floor
plan for a Standard No. 2. If the employee had a
large family, the living room might double as an
additional bedroom. Author's collection.

The Toledo & North Western, part of the sprawling Chicago & North Western system, erected a
Standard No. 2 depot in the north-central Iowa
farming community of Farnhamville more than
a century ago. John P. Vander Maas collection.

catalogs. Perhaps architectural standardization reached its zenith when prefabricated
houses, churches, and even hotels, privies, and playhouses could be ordered by mail for
shipment to virtually any location. These trends showed up particularly in the West. Hamlin Garland noted those "flimsy little wooden towns" on the Dakota prairie where elevators,
stores, houses, and depots, too, shared a depressing sameness. Put more bluntly, a Boston
businessman writing in the 1890s observed, "After spending months traveling through Dakota, Wyoming Terr., Colorado and Nebraska, I am struck by the poor quality of most
buildings. . . . Small stations especially are often of the dullest and most despicable types. I
saw few elegant and commodious stations while in this rather unpleasing part of the Re-
public." He then remarked that "there are wonderful ones east of the Missouri R. . . .
I suppose a railway company . . . cannot afford to spend large sums for such accommodations and the absence or rather reduction in this item of expenditure is one of the causes
why railroads out there have such poor buildings for the public."[27]

The visitor from Boston correctly sensed why "dull" railroad structures appeared.
Companies could not afford to erect expensive, architecturally distinctive, charming buildings in largely unsettled or undersettled areas; after all, west of the 100th meridian rail lines
frequently preceded population. This environment differed dramatically from most of the

East where the majority of towns existed before the coming of the rails. Carriers there could predict the traffic potential of each station. But this was not usually the case in the West. Railroads regularly entered the townsite business and planned communities every 5 to 15 miles along their lines. The economic prospects of such places were uncertain. While roads painted glowing pictures of these "New Edens" and "New Chicagos" through their townsite agents and in close conjunction with local boosters, the hard reality dictated that a sizable number of these raw villages were destined to remain whistle-stops. Town promotion was risky. Western roads, often short of funds because of construction and equipment costs, did not want to invest heavily in a depot for a new settlement that might fail. Similarly, they did not desire one that would exceed local needs. No wonder that as late as the eve of World War I, managers of the Santa Fe, officially the Atchison, Topeka & Santa Fe Railway, stated that their road "builds frame stations only on new lines and replaces them as soon as the community develops sufficiently to demand it. The structures range in size from 16 ft. by 40 ft. to 24 ft. by 65 ft. and 24 ft. by 80 ft. and cost about $1,200, $2,200 and $3,000 respectively. No frame structures are built, however, to replace existing structures."[28]

Closely related to cost considerations in explaining the dullness of depots in the West was convenience. A railroad's central or divisional offices could have a set of standard drawings for various sizes of stations, real or anticipated. The structures engineer of the Pierre, Rapid City & North Western Railway (popularly dubbed "Pretty Rough Country & No Water"), a satellite of the Chicago & North Western, commented on the subject after the completion of that 168-mile line in the West River Country of South Dakota in 1907: "It became a simple task for us to use . . . the standard Chicago & North Western combination passenger and freight station with living rooms for [an] agent on the second floor. . . ."[29]

But before the Rapid City road's "B&B" (bridge and building) gangs could construct depots, they placed portable structures at several locations that required agents immediately after the line opened for revenue service. Midland, for one, had received what was probably a boxcar body by the time the first train arrived on December 17, 1906. Often roads constructed to standard plans tiny, narrow buildings that, like the car body at Midland, could be moved easily by flatcar from station to station. The design philosophy was simple. "If the townsite makes it," observed an official of the Burlington & Missouri River Railroad in Nebraska, "residents will get [a regular] depot." Midland was growing and B&B carpenters soon finished a two-story depot based on a Chicago & North Western standard design.[30]

The use of portables was less troublesome and expensive than moving larger depots. Yet this happened. The Santa Fe, for instance, hauled by flatcar a two-story 24′ × 40′ standard wooden depot with living quarters the 24 miles from Las Cruces, New Mexico, to

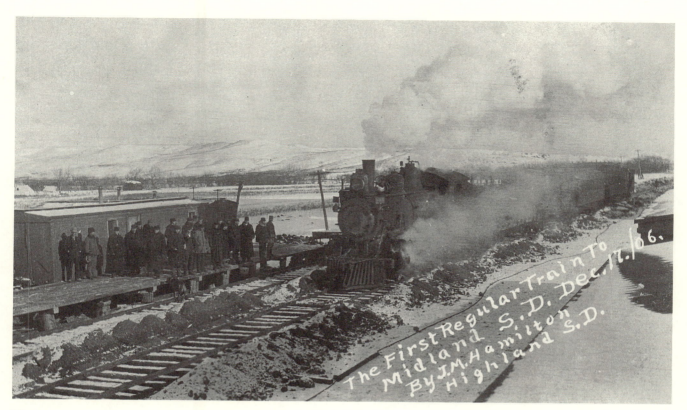

The First Regular Train To Midland S. D. Dec. 17, /06. By J.M. Hamilton, Highland S.D.

The first scheduled passenger train steams into the Chicago & North Western station at Midland, South Dakota, on December 17, 1906. In the railroad's rush to provide service, it employed a temporary depot. Soon thereafter, company carpenters assembled a two-story frame structure with upstairs apartment space, a necessity in this raw frontier village. John P. Vander Maas collection.

La Tuna (later Anthony), Texas, in 1910. The former station required a roomier structure while the latter needed what the Las Cruces one provided.[31]

Many communities, however, never saw a portable structure as did Midland and La Tuna, whether with or without an agent's apartment. Roads erected permanent depots during the line-construction phase, but ones that could be expanded easily if business increased. The depot-building practices of the Soo Line reveal a carrier that preferred combination depots with living quarters and structures that could be enlarged inexpensively and conveniently. Although the company used several types of standard plans, its most popular, Standard Second Class, appeared so widely along its far-flung system from Michigan to Montana that for decades it was a visual symbol of the road, a kind of three-dimensional logo. For instance, the company built more than two hundred of these buildings in North Dakota between 1891 and 1920.[32]

The Second Class Soo Line depot included traditional combination parts. The basic structure measured 24′ × 32′ and included the ticket office, separate "men's" and "ladies'" waiting rooms, and a small "warm room" to protect perishable freight (frequently beer) from the cold, a feature common to depots in the Northern Plains and Canada. A single-story freight room, usually 24 or 48 feet in length, extended from the end of the two-story core, thus making overall lengths of 56 and 80 feet. The size of the freight room was commensurate initially with the amount of business the Soo anticipated in the community. For example, the Second Class depot the company placed at Carrington, North Dakota, in 1892 measured 80 feet in length. But business subsequently boomed, so carpenters extended the freight house in 1902 and 1908 to a final length of 136 feet, revealing the adaptability of this popular design.[33]

The second-floor layout was simple. A stairway connected the ground-floor office with the upstairs living quarters. From the top of this passageway, a hall led to a 12′ × 17′ living room at one corner of the front, and a small 6′6″ × 13′6″ bedroom occupied the other trackside corner. A 12′ × 14′ kitchen and a 10′ × 13′ bedroom covered the back. As these structures were remodeled, variations occurred. As late as 1945, the Soo Line used a version of the Second Class depot at Max, North Dakota, to replace a 24′ × 80′ Second Class one that had burned in September 1944. This time, though, the company added a furnace room on the ground floor and reduced the freight section by 18 feet. But like the original structure, the replacement lacked an indoor toilet.[34]

Generally superior to the Soo Line's ubiquitous Second Class depots were the two-story ones erected by the sprawling Canadian Pacific and Canadian National systems and two of the latter's gargantuan predecessors, the Canadian Northern and the Grand Trunk Pacific. These carriers required thousands of depots, the majority of which contained living quarters. This was understandable since these companies opened tens of thousands of square miles to settlement, and nonrailroad housing was frequently limited or nonexistent. Sensitive to employees' needs, these railroads typically offered more spacious and convenient apartments than did carriers below the 49th parallel.

The depot design practices of the Canadian Northern Railway (CNoR) illustrate the nature of the two-story structures with agents' apartments in Canada. Early in the century this predominantly grain-gathering road developed a set of standard combination plans and extensively used its Third Class design. Constructed in several versions at more than three hundred small-town locations in Ontario, the Prairie Provinces, and British Columbia, this two-story edifice possessed striking qualities. Its high hip roof, prominent front and back gable dormers, and easily expandable single-story freight house became a company trademark that often stood out on the flat or gently rolling landscape. Indeed, these CNoR Third

The Soo Line depot at Max, North Dakota, is a second-generation building, constructed in 1945 to replace one that had burned. As late as the mid-1940s at least one American railroad valued an agent-occupied station. Author's collection.

Class structures were considerably more attractive than the Soo Line's Second Class ones with their gable roofs and plain lines.[35]

The floor plan of the Canadian Northern Third Class depot likewise offered pleasingly divergent features. In addition to the office, waiting room, and "freight shed" in this 45′ × 20′ structure, the company placed apartment space on both floors. This plan included a 21′10″ × 9′7″ kitchen annex which jutted out behind the building. The kitchen had doors that opened into the living room and to the outside and two opposing windows for cross ventilation. A stairway led from one end of the living room to four upstairs bedrooms, three of which measured approximately 12′ × 10′ each and a less spacious room measuring

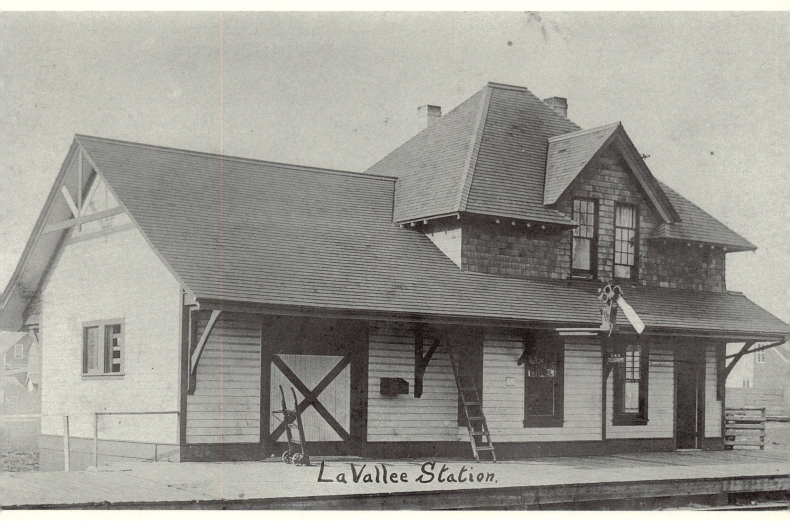

A *Third Class Canadian Northern depot stands at LaVallee, Ontario, on the railroad's Fort Frances–Winnipeg main line. This "real-photo" postcard dates from about 1907, the year the company erected this standardized structure. Author's collection.*

8'10" × 7'. While the Third Class depot was compact, it held approximately 750 square feet of living space, about 150 square feet more than the Soo Line's Second Class structure.[36]

When the Canadian National (CN) emerged after World War I, this government-owned railroad realized the practicality of Canadian Northern Third Class depots. Faced with building scores of depots along hundreds of miles of new, mostly branch lines during the 1920s and always needing replacement structures, the CN, not surprisingly, used versions of its predecessor's popular plan. Subsequently, it devised its own Third Class drawings which the railroad employed as late as the 1940s.

The Canadian National used its Third Class design for the depot at Bonnyville, Alberta, in 1929. The absence of dormers gives this style a squarish appearance not found with the earlier Canadian Northern Third Class depots. John P. Vander Maas collection.

Agents and their families found the Canadian National Third Class depot sensibly arranged. The first floor resembled the prototype, with the living room and kitchen placed in a similar fashion, but it also included a separate dining room. While the upstairs continued to offer four bedrooms, including a small one, it now contained "ample" closet space. The size increased to approximately 1,000 square feet, and the CN commonly added a basement for the central heating plant, for additional storage, and to keep "winter winds from getting under the floors." Those who lived in these depots probably found them visually pleasing; their low hip roofs that covered the second story and hip rather than gable roofs over the freight house made for attractive buildings.[37]

Although Canadian-style depots appeared south of the border, including a few Canadian National Third Class structures in Minnesota, the concept of living quarters entirely on the ground floor was not unknown. The Union Pacific (UP), most notably, built numerous single-story depots in several Great Plains and western states. In Nebraska, for instance, it erected about forty of these structures statewide; those in the eastern part dotted primarily appendages while those in the west appeared along both main and branch lines, reflecting patterns of available housing. These UP depots lacked the spaciousness of the Canadian Northern and Canadian National Third Class depots. The UP's 24′ × 64′ combination plan placed the four-room, 475-square-foot apartment on the waiting-room side and isolated the living quarters from the office, freight house, and waiting room. "These were

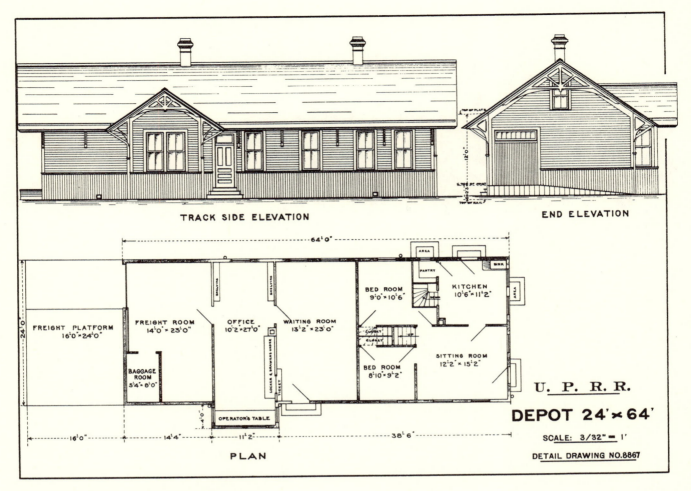

TRACK SIDE ELEVATION

END ELEVATION

PLAN

U. P. R. R.
DEPOT 24' × 64'
SCALE: 3/32" = 1'
DETAIL DRAWING NO. 8867

The mighty Union Pacific Railroad erected a number of depots with living quarters on the ground floor. This one-story standard 24' × 64' station was commonly selected for locations in Nebraska. Author's collection.

simple plans," remarked R. M. Brown, the company's chief engineer, in 1977. "We gave those agents only very basic housing."[38]

The reasons why the Union Pacific preferred a single-story design for depots with apartments can only be surmised. Likely several factors were involved. The bedrooms on the ground floor allowed occupants to escape a fire; absence of a stairway to climb repeatedly would be appealing, particularly on shopping-, wash-, or moving-day; and perhaps the design improved heating. The inconvenience of the door placements would discourage family members from interfering with the hustle and bustle of the station at train-time.

Still, the Union Pacific possessed two-story depots with living quarters. Mostly this happened through acquisition of other railroads. For example, the Oregon River & Navigation Company, which entered the UP orbit in 1898, owned a mixed lot of such buildings, several of which were large, ornate affairs. And a subsidiary, the Oregon Short Line, erected generally less fussy structures about the same time, mostly in eastern Idaho.[39]

In this process of expansion, the Union Pacific acquired a 70-mile short line, the Columbia Southern Railway, built during the late 1890s between the Oregon communities of Biggs and Shaniko and then leased in 1906 by the Oregon-Washington Railroad & Navigation Company, an affiliate of the UP. The Columbia Southern constructed a combination depot at Wasco that demonstrated that an American carrier could offer commodious accommodations. This structure consisted of two attached sections. The business portion, which measured approximately 40′ × 30′, contained typical components—waiting room, office, and freight room. Their positioning was unusual: passengers discovered that they could not walk directly from the waiting area to the platform. The agent, moreover, could not easily check the track because of the absence of a bay window. The apartment section, approximately 30′ × 23′, was much better conceived. The more than 1,100 square feet of floor space included three downstairs rooms—kitchen, dining room, and living room— and four upstairs bedrooms, two of which had attached closets. Like even the best depots of Canada, the one at Wasco lacked an indoor toilet. Yet unlike those structures north of the border, the Columbia Southern designed an austere exterior, having an almost Shaker-like quality. Simplicity of construction likely reduced building costs (the railroad was built on a shoestring); however, the availability of cheap local lumber surely explains its agreeable interior.[40]

More aesthetically inviting two-story depots with living quarters appeared in the West. When the Santa Fe early in the century constructed a strategic extension in eastern New Mexico to relieve a traffic bottleneck on its main line at Raton Pass, it faced the necessity of erecting more than a dozen combination depots. Engineers for the subsidiary that supervised the work, the Eastern Railway Company of New Mexico, logically decided to include an agent's apartment, "a consideration of some moment in the small New Mexico towns." The standard design called for customary upstairs accommodations: kitchen, living room, and two bedrooms. The anticipated heavy traffic on this Belen Cutoff may have prompted the railroad to isolate family members from this potential danger, not a concern for the Columbia Southern with its infrequent service.[41]

Erected in three sizes—24′ × 81′, the most popular, 24′ × 93′, and 24′ × 135′— in 1907 and 1908, these combination depots along the Belen Cutoff resembled other contemporary ones built in the region with their Mission Revival styling. What was unusual about them was their construction material. Rather than wood, the company selected concrete and stucco. "The climate of the country in which the Eastern Railway of New Mexico is located should make a concrete station most satisfactory," concluded *Railway Age* in 1906. "The generally dry atmosphere should prevent any possible 'sweating' of the walls, while the similarity in certain respects of concrete buildings and the adobe houses which are still common in New Mexico and most satisfactory to the inhabitants because of their

The former Columbia Southern depot in Wasco, Oregon, is seen in this mid-1950s photograph. Spartan on the exterior, the interior floor plan reveals ample living space. John P. Vander Maas collection. Robert H. Jones drawing.

SEPTEMBER 1900

Columbia Southern Railway Company

WASCO DEPOT

SCALE 1/4"=1'

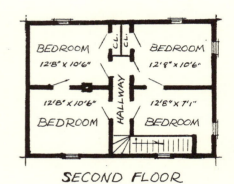

SECOND FLOOR

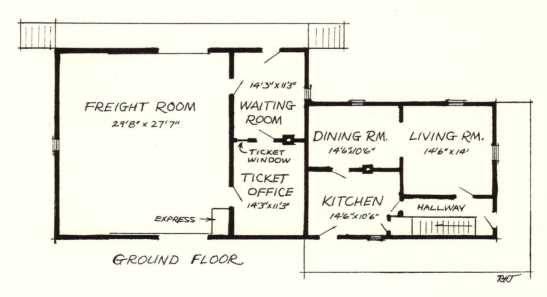

GROUND FLOOR

comparative coolness in the hot summer months and warmth in winter, indicates the qualities of comfort which a concrete depot should possess." There is no indication that the Santa Fe erred either in terms of using apartments or concrete.[42]

While the Santa Fe added to its inventory of standard two-story depots with living quarters early in the century, the Southern Pacific (SP), another powerful western road, revealed even more partiality to this depot type. Likewise committed to the economy and convenience of standard plans, the SP drew up nearly a dozen plans for two-story wooden combination depots with living quarters. They were placed along its lines from Oregon to Texas, especially in California. The company erected large numbers of two comparable designs, with customary variations: approximately fifty Benicia and more than sixty Standard No. 22 types. The former appeared mainly between 1888 and 1892, a time of considerable line construction, and the latter from 1899 to 1910. Henry E. Bender, Jr., the foremost student of SP standard depots, christened the Benicia style which honors the California community that received one of this type. The railroad, however, designated the second style as its Standard No. 22. "Because the official name of each of [the standard] designs . . . vanished in the smoking ruins of the SP's general office building during the 1906 San Francisco Earthquake and Fire," observed Bender, "the plans for the two standard depots that were being built at that time, Standard No. 22 and Standard No. 23 [a single-story combination depot without an apartment] were redrawn later in 1906, and the SP continued to build those two designs for a few years afterwards."[43]

The Southern Pacific Standard No. 22 rivals any other plan used in the United States for quality of external and internal features. While this design creates a simple gable roof, a rectangular bay extends from the central office past the upstairs living room which a cross-gable roof caps, thus considerably enhancing the building's appearance. The SP, furthermore, creatively organized the floor space. The 25′ × 32′ apartment included a living room (with the bay window), two bedrooms, kitchen, pantry, storeroom, and bath, the latter with toilet and tub. The nature of the structure allowed for major modifications. An agent at Goleta, California, for example, easily converted attic space above the baggage room and adjacent to the kitchen into an extra bedroom. "These were good looking depots," recalled a former SP official, "and they served our agents well." And he added, "The fact that we used so many of these number 22s attests to their aptness." The Western Pacific Railroad provides another testimonial. This company, which opened its main line between Oakland, California, and Salt Lake City, Utah, in 1910, when the Standard No. 22 plan was in vogue, replicated versions of the SP design at several locations.[44]

Providing housing for agents involved more than building depots with the popular upper-floor apartment. Several carriers—Illinois Central and Santa Fe are examples—built sepa-

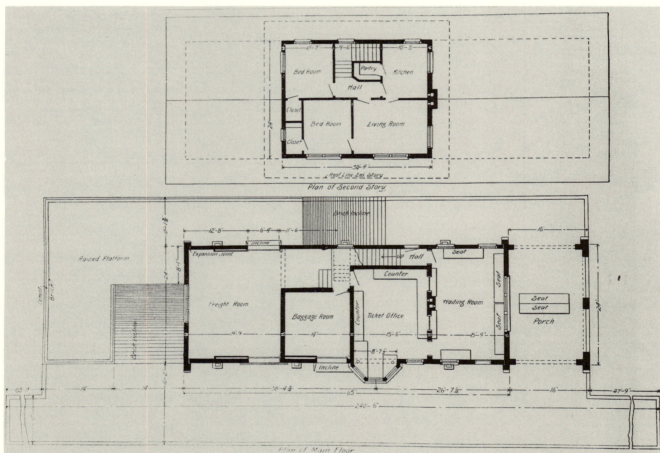

This artist's conception shows the nontrackside elevation of the standard Santa Fe Railway concrete depot, ca. 1906. Covered by galvanized iron roofs, these buildings contain rounded bays, brackets, and other minor decorative features. The Spanish-inspired flavor blends nicely into the local architectural landscape. These structures offer modest living accommodations. Author's collection.

When the Eastern Railway of New Mexico, a subsidiary of the Santa Fe, built its standard concrete and stucco depots, it constructed most to the scale used at Montainair, New Mexico, 24' x 81', but it selected a 24' x 93' size for Texico, New Mexico, a more important station. The New Mexico communities of Clovis, Melrose, and Vaughn saw similar depots, but they measured 24' x 135'. John P. Vander Maas collection.

During the late nineteenth century the Southern Pacific frequently used the plan for its depot at Benicia, California (seen in this July 1947 photograph). This predominately Stick-style architecture, with its second-story exterior covered with patterned shingles, made for an attractive trackside building. Twelve Benicia-design depots still stand, although none are used by the railroad. John P. Vander Maas collection.

rate cottages for agents and their families. They were generally roomier than comparable quarters in depots and further removed or protected families from trackside dangers. The costs of construction and maintenance, though, surely limited their usage. "If you have both a depot and an agent's house," argued an Union Pacific structures officer, "you will have much more to keep up."[45]

Railroads more commonly erected detached housing for their maintenance-of-way workers, and mostly for the same reasons that led to depot apartments. "It is very essential that the men employed on track-work live on their section, or as close to it as feasible, so as to be always on hand in case of emergencies and to avoid loss of time in going to and from their work," concluded the chief engineer of the Lehigh Valley Railroad in 1904. "Where the route of a railroad does not pass through thickly-settled districts, a railroad company is forced . . . to build special houses, known as 'section houses.'" Whether they accommodated one or more families or a number of workers, these section houses appeared throughout the United States and Canada. Also, railroads provided employees other than

SOU. PAC. DEPOT
GUADALUPE. CALIF.

A *fine example of the Southern Pacific Standard No. 22 depot is found at Guadalupe, California, on June 4, 1974. Not only was the structure constructed to a common design, but for years it sported standard "Southern Pacific Yellow" paint, which the company called "Colonial Yellow." A variety of colors graced the interior at different times, including the ubiquitous yellow, "Sash Green" (another standard color), and various browns and beiges. John P. Vander Maas collection.*

agents and section hands with housing, "especially at points where shops or junction stations are located at some distances from settlements."[46]

As the United States emerged from the terrible depression of the 1890s, a recently perfected form of intercity transport caught the public's eye. The electric interurban railway signaled a transportation advance that many thought would yield enormous benefits and economic opportunities. One enthusiast saw electric-powered railroads performing "a service for mankind as notable and perhaps ultimately as great as that rendered by its steam-powered precursor." Debuting as a 7-mile "rural trolley line" between the central Ohio communities of Newark and Granville in 1889, electric interurbans grew to a nationwide total of approximately 1,500 miles within a decade. By 1916 mileage peaked at 15,580, with approximately three hundred companies in operation. Although Ohio and Indiana were the heartland of the interurban, lines could be found connecting such remote places as Bisbee and Warren, Arizona, and Cripple Creek and Victor, Colorado. Mileage in Canada reached 850 by World War I, although that country's twenty-five carriers, unlike many in the United States, were almost entirely isolated from one another.[47]

Building patterns similar to what occurred with steam railroads took place on American and Canadian electric interurban railways. Companies recycled existing structures with living space, built specially designed ones with agents' quarters, and erected similar facilities from standard plans. Interurbans, too, occasionally constructed dwellings and dormitories for employees.[48]

Hundreds of depots—some merely cheaply built shelters—sprang up along interurban routes. Initially, the industry relied heavily on existing structures, often storefront offices and former private dwellings. These facilities generally worked well because electric roads nearly always entered the community's commercial core, providing riders and shippers of express and less-than-carload freight with downtown-to-downtown service.

More successful interurbans erected substantial structures of their own design, some of which contained living quarters. The large roads might erect urban passenger and freight terminals and, less frequently, two-story storefront depots. The latter offered curbside office and waiting-room space and spacious upstairs living accommodations. Interurbans, however, more commonly built dual depots and electrical substations. Often of brick and concrete construction to reduce the risk of fire, some included apartment space. These "juice" roads discovered that employees who lived in such places performed well. The Minneapolis-based Twin City Rapid Transit Company, which exhibited characteristics of both a street railway and an interurban, concluded that an operator on the premises "is able to give better supervision to the station and is available for emergency calls without delay."[49]

Hammered by automobile, bus, and truck competition by the 1920s, the interurban industry collapsed before additional, specially designed depots, including any with operators' quarters, appeared. Yet what happened in electric traction early in the twentieth century paralleled the evolution of depots built by steam roads during the nineteenth century: hit-or-miss eclectic architecture evolved into standardized varieties with the recurring notion that living in the depot might be an appropriate part of such structures.

THE AGENT AND THE DEPOT

The experience of living in the depot is remembered differently by thousands of employees and their families. Nonetheless, a near consensus exists that where acute housing shortages occurred, an apartment over a depot far surpassed the common alternatives: living in a cramped bunkcar, old passenger coach, hotel room, or more likely a rooming house or boardinghouse.

Admittedly, the rooming house or boardinghouse might be more satisfactory for unmarried railroaders, agents, telegraphers, trainmen, and the like. An itinerant "boomer" brakeman recalled in the 1920s his earlier experiences on the Toledo, St. Louis & Western Railroad, the Clover Leaf Route. "Now I remember I paid two dollars a week for my room and two bits a meal at the boarding house where I lived at there in Frankfort [Indiana], and like most all boarding houses in those days, it had a saloon in connection with it, and the barroom was right joining the big dining room, and in the dining room there were two big long tables, where the food was put on in family style, and you could help yourself and eat all you wanted, and us boys while in off the road would loaf around in the barroom and play cards, checkers, and dominoes for little brass checks, which were good at the bar."[1]

The boardinghouse posed serious drawbacks for an agent with a spouse and children. Not only might it be uncomfortably crowded, but in an era when people were keenly sensitive to the "liquor question," a saloon of sorts on the premises would be unthinkable. The "drys" wanted exposure only to water, or "Adam's ale," and other nonalcoholic beverages. Moreover, hotels, rooming houses, and boardinghouses often charged more for their services than a small-town station agent could afford for an extended stay with dependents.

Even if the rooming house or boardinghouse offered no impediments in terms of space, alcohol, and cost, other factors might make such accommodations difficult. An agent-telegrapher for the Minneapolis & St. Louis Railway (M&StL) who was single and worked in the village of Middle Grove, Illinois, discovered troublesome housing as late as the 1930s. His experiences with "Mabel," whom he described as a "grass widow in her 30's," graphically illustrate the limitations of this type of living arrangement.

There is no mistaking that the Baltimore & Ohio depot at Folsom, Pennsylvania, on the road's Baltimore to Philadelphia line, also serves as a residence. This ca. 1919 view, taken by a company photographer, reveals a more sophisticated design than that commonly found in other sections of the country. The hip roof, shed dormers, and porte cochere or carriage porch suggest the handiwork of Frank Furness (1839–1912), Philadelphia's dominant architect of the late nineteenth century, the time when the B&O entered southeastern Pennsylvania. Similar depots appeared at Darby, Pennsylvania, and Carrcroft, Delaware. B&O Railroad Museum, courtesy of H. H. Harwood, Jr.

My first impression of Mabel's house, which was badly in need of paint, could have been better. Not modern in any way, it consisted of three rooms downstairs—kitchen, living room and bedroom, and there were probably two rooms upstairs, but I never knew for sure, never having been above the ground floor.

While being shown through the house, it was necessary to walk around a washing machine standing in the kitchen filled with used wash water, and as if Mabel had been interrupted in her work, a dish pan filled with soapy water and dirty dishes on the coal range, but as long as I stayed there, possibly six months, neither of these household items ever looked any different—always full. . . .

Taking a bath posed [a] . . . problem. There being no bathroom, the logical place for the wash tub would have been in front of the warm kitchen range. However, there were no doors to shut the kitchen from the rest of the house, leaving only one other place—the garage, a building that had seen better days.[2]

Living in the depot did not mean luxurious conditions. Just as "Mabel's" roomer coped with the absence of modern plumbing, often so did those who inhabited these railway structures. The Southern Pacific, for one, initially provided water to the building and later sanitary facilities. The Soo Line, more representative, took years to supply water and toilets, and at many places it never did. Station occupants therefore trudged to smelly, remote outhouses or used somewhat more convenient chamber pots. They lugged pails of water from an outside pump up the stairway to the kitchen for their cooking and bathing. Some companies placed cisterns under their depots and connected them to upstairs pumps. "We had a cistern under the basement which we had water hauled into," recalled a onetime resident of the Minneapolis & St. Louis depot in Madison, Minnesota. "The pump (hand pump) was in the kitchen by the sink. This water was just used for washing, and we hauled all our drinking water in glass jugs."[3]

When placed in perspective, station residents frequently were not initially worse off than their neighbors. In communities where two-story depots predominated, public water and sewer systems often did not appear until the second, third, or fourth decades of the twentieth century. But by the post–World War II years, these services had become commonplace, even in the smallest villages. Agents and their families by then had reason to howl if they still lacked these advantages.

Depot residents made other complaints about their accommodations. "One problem in those typical two-story depots was what to do with a piano," remembered Lloyd Reeves, whose family lived in several Chicago, Burlington & Quincy stations in Nebraska. "My dad played the piano. But there was no way to get one up to the second floor. Maybe Dad found a spot in the waiting room or in the freight room." The stairway itself was not only a roadblock for some personal possessions but also a nuisance, necessitating awkward climbs carrying water, coal, laundry, and household supplies. Parents understandably encouraged their children to help. "When I got older it was me and my brother's job to pack the coal and kindling upstairs for the stove for which we received an allowance of 15 cents per week," remembered the former inhabitant of the Chicago & North Western depot at Crocker, Iowa. "Also on washday we had to pack the water up for mom to do the wash." Dale Reeves, the older brother of Lloyd, recollected that "there was a 'coal house,' . . . across the side-track behind the depot, where we went to get coal for the stove and coal oil for the lamps. There was a wood-pile next to the coal house, where my dad and I chopped wood."[4]

While youngsters might assist with household and depot chores, the station setting posed physical harm to them. The movement of freight and passenger trains, even on lightly used branch lines, could be deadly for a toddler who strayed onto the track. Older children, too, might neglect to heed rolling stock being switched or fail to hear a steam locomotive coming. "Locomotives could sneak up on even an adult," remarked a veteran station agent. "They weren't always that noisy." Dale Reeves recalled the dangers and why they especially troubled his mother. "My mother hated the depot. She worried about me and my brother and sister. The platform and the tracks were our playground, and the trains on the main line provided a frequent, serious threat." His mother's concerns were real. "Youngsters were easily injured falling when running across the tracks. I once tripped with my toes on one rail and made a one-point landing on my jaw against the other rail. My jaw wasn't broken, but I was in pain and couldn't eat for awhile." And Reeves concluded, "Years later, when I wanted to reminisce, my mother would not discuss our days in depots. She never overcame the dread of tracks and trains."[5]

The station environment seemed conducive to juvenile mischief, including the potentially lethal variety. "I think that kids living and playing around the depot had some golden opportunities to get themselves into a peck of trouble," opined one former railroader. And he was correct if the autobiographical remarks of the son of a Milwaukee Road agent are typical. Born on the second-floor of the depot at Chatsworth, Iowa, this individual recollected events from the six years he spent in this place as a child.

> The depot was up on piling so platform would be level with the floor of a passenger coach. Recall that I swiped one of my Dad's "seegars" out of a box in his desk; smoked it under the depot. They found me three hours later, still green (and other colors) "around the gills." The Wells Fargo Express Co. furnished a huge revolver for use when shipment of money in the depot. It was kept in a top drawer of the ticket counter. It fascinated me. I spent hours just gazing at it but stood on notice that I'd "get my ribs kicked in" if I ever so much as touched it.

> I also recall that a long hose was attached to the bottom of the locomotive water tank at one end of the station platform. Somehow I managed to get the loose end of it into the basement window of a house across the tracks from the depot. Filled it with 2 ft. of water. I got a dusting with a real sturdy stick. Never heard if it was on account of wasting locomotive water or filling the basement. Likely a combination of both?[6]

Although the job of station agent never ranked high on the list of dangerous occupations, agents and their families faced some risks with their trackside homes. The most common involved fire. These typically wooden structures, with their open-flame illumination (likely prior to 1900) and coal and wood stoves, abutting the path of spark-throwing steam locomotives, burned with some frequency. In North Dakota, for example, flames totally engulfed twenty-five in-service Soo Line depots between 1889 and 1976. While fire protection existed in most communities, volunteer brigades were notoriously ineffective, and "these frame stations were usually at the mercy of the flames." No wonder maintenance-of-way workers commonly nailed emergency ladders to the sides of occupied structures and agents often kept buckets of water and glass fire grenades handy. While data on injury and loss of life by fire of inhabited depots are unavailable, fire was, according to the superintendent of the Norfolk, Nebraska–based Eastern Division of the Chicago & North Western in the 1920s, "a matter of great concern." Much less common than conflagrations, but not unknown, were injuries and deaths caused by train wrecks and even by an avalanche. The latter smashed the Canadian Pacific depot at Rogers, British Columbia, in January 1899, instantly killing the agent and his young family.[7]

Admittedly trains did not often jump the track in front of depots, but, of course, they passed them regularly. A frequent visitor to the Chicago, Burlington & Quincy depot at Berwyn, Nebraska, during the 1930s recalled that it was "very strange to live that close to the tracks" and that it was "quite an experience when the trains went past—the noise and the place kind of shook." The raucous passing annoyed residents, too. "I never really got used to all of that noise," remembered the daughter of an agent for the Chicago & North Western in South Dakota. "The piercing cry of the whistle, the clanging bell, the squeaking wheels and the monster locomotive itself would give you a good startle in the middle of the night and might keep you awake." And she added, "A stopping passenger train always seemed to be especially loud, with the mail, baggage and express being worked and the passengers coming and going. There weren't any 'Please Be Quiet' signs on the platform!" Actually, some residents might be affected by the *lack* of noise. The wife of the Southern Pacific agent at Goleta, California, recalled that "it was the silence caused by the train that did not arrive on time that was most likely to wake one up from a sound sleep."[8]

The negative side of station life also included the likelihood of cold and drafty conditions during winter months, a drawback more constant than the occasional excessive noise. These wooden depots generally lacked insulation of any type, and if they received such upgrading, it customarily came after World War I. To keep structures warmer and also to lower maintenance costs, the Canadian Pacific and the Soo Line, for example, covered their depots with a type of asphalt siding sold under the trademark of Insul-brick (the name came from the product's purported insulating properties and the bricklike outlines stamped on one side of each panel), while the Canadian National preferred the application of a coating of stucco. Other roads in the colder climes selected asphalt siding or stucco or perhaps filled hollow depot walls with granulated rock wool. Some agents, either in their desire to winterize or for convenience, threw old papers—tariffs, timetables, waybills, and the like—and other trash behind freight-room walls. Companies might also add storm windows and doors and skirting around the foundations, and if they did not, agents might make these improvements at their own expense. But as buildings aged, the fight against the elements seemed more difficult, and it was never fully won.[9]

A *crowd gathers at the Illinois Central's station in Archer, Iowa, at train-time early in the century. The wooden ladder, attached to the side of the two-story depot, could be used for fire-fighting and fire-escape purposes. John P. Vander Maas collection.*

In 1907 a westbound freight train on the Boston & Albany Railroad derailed at West Brimfield, Massachusetts, 78 miles west of Boston. According to a note on the back of the photograph: "A narrow escape for the Agent & his family who lived upstairs over the station." Louis W. Goodwin collection.*

The agent at the Chicago, Burlington & Quincy Railroad (Burlington Route) depot at Eckley, Colorado, attempted to reduce the chilling effects of winter winds with plastic window coverings. Although this photograph dates from 1954, the station grounds still contain the outside privy. John P. Vander Maas collection.

If agents upgraded their apartment space, they nearly always sustained the costs. Their improvements might include kitchen cabinets, light fixtures, and floor coverings. When they left, some agents removed or tore out their contributions if their successors refused to reimburse them. Some, too, might want to use these betterments in their new abodes. Remembered the son of an agent from Minnesota, "It was a nuisance to have to take these things." In addition, "You might well find a depot that was really messed up by the previous tenant tearing off the wallpaper, taking out shelves or whatever. . . . There might have been some person who had gone wild with the paint brush, covering everything with a strange color of paint."[10]

Another disadvantage of depot apartments involved their compact size. As indicated, floor plans usually included only two small bedrooms. Exceptions occurred, with the principal ones being found in the Canadian West. But families during the nineteenth and early twentieth centuries ordinarily had more than one or two children. To rectify the paucity of space, living rooms or even kitchens turned into sleeping quarters at night or space on the ground floor was used for sleeping. Carriers might be helpful; the Canadian Pacific aided at least one employee. "When the family of the caretaker agent at St. Lazare, Quebec, began expanding," noted Toronto writer Ron Brown, "the CPR simply severed off a piece of the waiting room to create a third bedroom. By his retirement in 1942 the family numbered eight; and the station had been significantly enlarged."[11]

No amount of adaptation or remodeling could assuage the psychological pain caused by intense isolation. Obviously, this was not a problem in a Connecticut or Pennsylvania location, but it might be one in Alberta or New Mexico. Some stations were not part of bona fide communities but rather stood in remote locations to serve the needs of a shipper

The Burlington Route erected a standard-type depot in the lonely, high plains village of Peetz, Colorado, at the turn of the century. The agent wished to improve the station's appearance, as is evident with the picket fence and trellis. A child's bicycle and perhaps the family dog are included in this March 5, 1955, image. John P. Vander Maas collection.

or for train-control purposes. Living in such a place meant little contact with the outside world. Mail and supplies came by rail as did specially designed school and medical cars. Later, however, radio, both commercial and private, and all-weather roads lessened but never fully ended the solitude.[12]

If agents lived and worked in isolation, they experienced little pestering from patrons. But most who called the depot home met the public constantly, and this could be disruptive and annoying. "Many times people would come down to the depot after supper at 7 or 8 P.M.," reflected the son of an agent who lived in a North Western depot, "and ask my dad to deliver an express or freight shipment to them. A lot of them were farmers that worked all day in the fields. My dad always done it without complaining as he felt that was part of his job." That feeling of responsibility was more likely to occur before World War II. After that time the Order of Railway Telegraphers, the principal labor union for station agents, flexed its collective muscles and pressed hard for overtime pay and annual paid vacations. "No '8-hour law' in those olden days," recalled a longtime agent. "My Dad [an agent for the Milwaukee], like all R.R. men worked endless hours, 7 days a week, 365 days a year. If they 'went railroading' they expected to."[13]

While no railroad job, including that of a live-in agent, produced total satisfaction, pleasant aspects to the work and life existed. No one disagreed that employees and family members were associated with an occupation that had exciting and enjoyable dimensions. "The folks there at the railroad station were the center of town life," recalled a woman who spent her childhood in a village in the central part of South Dakota. "We kids were really proud that our father was the agent and telegraph operator there." And she added, "He was important and so we thought that we were too!"[14]

The physical setting of the station helped to enhance its importance and that of its occupants. Admittedly, the structure at times might be located away from the existing town if the iron horse arrived after settlement occurred. In the East places with "depot" or "station" in their names might spring up a mile or more from long-established towns of the same names. Connecticut, for example, had Mansfield Depot, Stepney Depot, and Washington Depot, which served their namesake communities. Railroads missed these towns usually because they straddled hilltops or ridges; surveyors selected the more practical valleys for their rights-of-way. Where the railroad preceded the town, the station commonly stood in the heart of the community. On the Great Plains hundreds of settlements were laid out by townsite companies, often corporate subsidiaries of the carriers themselves, in such a fashion as to set the depot at the head of the future "main drag." "Main Street began at the tracks," explained geographer John C. Hudson, "creating an arrangement in which the railroad formed the bar of a T-shaped configuration." These "T-towns" meant that the community's principal roadway stopped directly at the depot's backdoor, and commercial structures appeared close-by. "The 'crossed T' form was a better anchor on business locations and produced a tighter cluster nearest the center." The depot stood literally in the thick of things, a more prominent location than most other buildings and unquestionably more so than a doctor's house or preacher's manse.[15]

Like the centrality of the depot, the railroad agent stood in the community's limelight. As the official local representative of the railroad before the demise of the small-town station (except for some that served commuters), he, and occasionally she, was probably as well known in community life as the physician and preacher. The reasons are many. Agents or operators met the public when they sold tickets, planned travel itineraries, and reported shipments of express and freight. Some, too, peddled oddments, including postcards, stationery, and spool thread.[16]

Even if individuals traveled little and seldom sent or received goods, they surely had contact with the agent. Occasionally the person at the depot served as the town's reader. Individuals who could not read knew that the agent could. "If any reading matters came their way, they usually headed to the depot to have it interpreted." More significantly, the agent acted as the conduit for incoming and outgoing messages. With firsthand knowledge of the cryptic Morse code, the agent was the best informed person in town. The telegraph carried more than routine railroad business (train movements, switch lists, and the like); it transmitted commercial messages from one of the several private telegraph companies, including the largest and most famous, Western Union. (By the turn of the century the distinctive blue-and-white porcelain signs that announced "WESTERN UNION TELEGRAPH and CABLE OFFICE" were attached to thousands of American depots.) Before long-distance telephone calls became possible and then popular, a person who wished to communicate quickly with someone out of town sent a wire. Even the community newspaper depended heavily on the agent's telegraphic abilities. As the daughter of an Iowa newspaper editor recalled, "The [agent] was truly our link with national events, for in those days before radio and television the telegrapher got everything first, including the weather forecast. My father haunted the depot for these forecasts as well as important world events." Naturally, an agent who actually lived in the depot, "always a beehive of activity," was all the more prominent.[17]

While children could claim that they were the son or daughter of a "sure enough big shot," they also took pleasure in other aspects of station life. Most youngsters struck up

Station, Oak River, Man.

This picture postcard, perhaps sold by the Canadian Pacific agent at Oak River, Manitoba, shows this uniformed company representative and also three small children who are dangerously close to the tracks. Louis W. Goodwin collection.

friendships with train crews, and this meant opportunities to ride in the cab of a mighty locomotive and maybe take the throttle for a few minutes. "Pure fascination is what those steamers held for me," related the son of a Southern Pacific agent from California. "My brother and I could usually hitch a short ride in the cab but usually no other kid there in San Dimas was so lucky. That sure swelled our heads. . . . That was something else." These depot children enjoyed playing on the tracks. "We could jump from one rail to the other parallel rail and maintain very good balance. Also, if we happened to have a penny, we'd sometimes lay it on the rail to see how the train would flatten it." And "depot kids" magnetically attracted their peers. The children of John Mason, who lived in the Canadian National station at Stouffville, Ontario, during the 1910s and 1920s, remembered that "climbing the old wooden water tower was a favourite sport." They further recalled that "the hand-operated turntable was usually covered with children taking rides while others pushed."[18]

There were always occasions for children to gaze out of upstairs windows at wondrous sights. They loved to observe the ritual of a passenger train's arrival, undoubtedly a high point in the daily routine of community life. One person's most vivid memory from childhood involved such an event. "It was . . . fun to watch out my bedroom window at nite to see people getting on or off the train not over 25–30 feet away." Moreover, the two-story depot, likely the tallest structure locally except perhaps for ubiquitous grain elevators and the railroad's water tank, gave its occupants a grand view of the hinterlands. The comments of H. A. Stimson capture the joy he found from his lofty vantage point. "From our second story view I could see farms, buildings and dust in the distance. A farmer coming to town with oxen and a stone boat could be seen a mile away. Such a conveyance beckoned to me and I would jog out to meet him and play train coming in by jumping on and off the deck." The excitement could continue. "A wagon outfit angling across the prairie indicated something out of the ordinary which called for my investigation. Often this turned out to be some frugal farmer bringing in a load of buffalo bones [to sell for carbon black or fertilizer] which were everywhere over the unplowed prarie [sic]. I felt I was doing something big loading a pelvic bone that had sun dried to the point that it likely weighed less than ten pounds." [19]

While Stimson was the quintessential boy, girls, too, had many gratifying experiences while living at trackside. The adjacent right-of-way of the Minneapolis & St. Louis Railway in western Minnesota appealed to Gwen Hurd Hempel, who discovered a seasonal pleasure. "For me and my young friends the railroad tracks were a wonderful source of purple violets in the springtime (we marveled that they could grow out of the cinder beds). Also, our high school botany class made field trips for wild flowers along the tracks." [20]

Railroading, however, was mostly a male world. While carriers had female agents-operators, more likely custodians, they were exceptional. Boys and not usually girls considered the possibility of a career in station service. If they were the son of an agent and lived in the depot, they had "a leg up on the other youngsters." They could master the rudiments of bookkeeping, telegraphy, and other requisite skills. "These lads were able to learn a trade without cost and without having to live away from home while doing so, then step into a job . . . in one of the most interesting industries in the world." If wives or daughters possessed these talents and if their husbands or fathers died suddenly, they might win temporary or perhaps permanent positions, especially during times of labor shortages. "For some women who knew telegraphy and station-keeping, it was sure better than having a life insurance policy on the departed bread winner, which usually meant a decent funeral and burial for him but not much else." [21]

Depot housing was convenient, of course, even essential for living in some localities. But it also held financial advantages for the agent. Railroads did not customarily charge for these accommodations, although they might eventually as other properties became readily available. Even then rents were modest. The companies also provided free utilities, and this meant that coal for heating and cooking and oil for lamps were complementary. Cost considerations were weighed carefully. For example, when assigned by the Burlington Route to Wolbach, Nebraska, on its remote Palmer-Burwell branch during World War II, the Reeves family knew that they could live rent-free in the old frame depot. "That was a big decision before we moved." But the parents preferred a house. "The folks ended up renting the Methodist Church parsonage. Rent was only $7 per month and was apparently worth the cost."[22]

In a related example, the question of whether to pay monthly rent received attention when an agent considered "bidding-in" on a station that lacked the rent-free benefit. When the father of H. A. Stimson told family members early in the century that he could leave the hamlet of Canistota, South Dakota, and its two-story depot for the junction point of Iroquois, 60 miles and seven stations up the Chicago & North Western's Iowa and Dakota Line, and one lacking living quarters in its depot, this conversation took place:

"Do you want to move?" Dad asked quietly as he sampled the food on the dinner table.

"Move where—when—why?" we chorused.

"Iroquois is open and I can have it. Pays more, but will have to pay rent. Ten regular trains but there is a clerk-operator."[23]

The senior Stimson took the job. The greater wages compensated for the end of rent- and utility-free housing, and the family luckily found an affordable dwelling several blocks from the station. And Mrs. Stimson welcomed the chance for a better social life; "she had never been much of a mixer in Canistota."[24]

The Reeves and Stimsons could afford private housing, but during hard times employees and furloughed workers might take refuge in depots, even those that were never designed for habitation. Because sharp cutbacks in the work force after the Crash of 1929 prompted railroaders to "bump" others with less seniority, some had no alternative but to accept low-paying jobs. These unlucky individuals might opt for depot living to make ends meet. The saga of the five-member Garwick family illustrates what happened. "Papa worked for the Rock Island Railroad, and to keep his seniority rights when the Depression hit, he had to take a custodial-type job in New Liberty, Iowa," remembered family member Kenneth Garwick. In 1932 the family moved to this northeastern Iowa village along the Rock Island's freight-only Clinton branch. "We lived in the [combination] depot rent free, had coal furnished for heating and cooking, plus $25.00 per month for taking care of two freight trains a day. The depot consisted of a waiting room, which was our living [room] and bedroom. The ticket office was our kitchen and the freight room was used for our

Model-A Ford, if there was room." With a trackside vegetable garden, several goats, odd jobs, and that modest monthly check, the Garwicks eked out an existence until better times returned in 1938. Garwick found a more attractive position with the Rock Island, so the family left the depot at New Liberty to the care of a local custodian.[25]

Similarly, former employees might occupy depots, usually ones without agents or custodians. A laid-off Minneapolis & St. Louis Railway section hand with a large family squatted for most of the Great Depression in the derelict depot at Elrick Junction, Iowa, located in the southeastern part of the state. The station once served the Muscatine, Burlington & Southern Railroad, an abandoned short line, and the M&StL. The latter by the 1930s used the structure to store track-maintenance equipment; its intended purpose as an interchange facility had passed. M&StL officials ignored their uninvited tenants at Elrick Junction, probably feeling pity toward them and knowing that their tools were safe.[26]

Living in the depot declined steadily after World War II. The end of wartime rationing, including gasoline and tires, greater availability of reliable automobiles, and an extensive system of all-weather roads gave agents greater options for housing. "The car really freed the agent from staying in the depot if he thought there was a need to find better housing," noted a former agent. "Sure there was a price to pay, the cost of rent or buying a house and the commuting. But some fellows didn't worry much about those things. They just wanted something better like living in a county seat town with its better shopping and better schools."[27]

If agents wished to remain in the depot, they still might be forced to relocate. For one thing, some carriers physically eliminated living quarters. Flush with funds after World War II and anxious to make their smaller depots more efficient and more maintenance free, they embarked on extensive programs of remodeling ("remuddling" from a preservationist's perspective). "The Howard [South Dakota] train depot was remodeled in 1956 providing a modern station for the Milwaukee Road," wrote a reporter for the nearby Huron newspaper. "The ancient two-story station was moved away and what was the freight house was remodeled for the new station."[28]

Moreover, railroads closed hundreds of these venerable abodes during the 1950s and 1960s. The explanation for this dramatic decline primarily involved obsolescence. Generally, small-town depots, whether occupied or not, no longer were necessary for railroad operations, except some for daily commuters and occasionally for office and storage purposes. Passenger trains vanished rapidly on branch lines after World War II, a victim of bus and most of all automobile competition. Furthermore, large sections of main lines, "high iron," became freight-only, even prior to the debut of Amtrak, the National Railroad Passenger Corporation, in 1971. A similar scenario occurred in Canada, although some agents continued to live in their depots there until the 1970s.

The fading of passenger service is only one of several factors that killed this genre of depot. The abandonment of trackage, especially branch and duplicate main lines—what the industry calls "plant rationalization"—has been ongoing in recent decades. It is a result of such forces as the negative economic impact of truck competition, frequent corporate mergers, and a more favorable regulatory climate. The American railway system dropped from 229,530 route miles in 1929 to only 116,626 in 1991, and the Canadian network contracted proportionally. With trackage gone, support installations became worthless. Railroad companies also have been able to abandon stations easier since the 1960s and, after 1980, with enactment of partial deregulation, could close them at will. From the 1960s on, carriers have argued effectively that they can serve freight customers through centralized agencies and more recently with toll-free telephone calls aided by computerized information about equipment and billings. Railroads, moreover, no longer handle less-than-carload freight and express, traffic that largely disappeared by the late 1960s. Also, modern dispatching, employing to various degrees Centralized Traffic Control (CTC), radios, and computers, has eliminated need for trackside reports from operators.[29]

Only a modest number of the several thousand two-story depots with living space remain. Some continue to serve carriers but as storage structures. A few stand abandoned. Most of these historic structures, however, have been recycled into restaurants, offices, museums, and other public places. Some are private homes.

What Tom Kelly did at Piermont, New York, is an extreme example of this process of adaptive use. Kelly was born in the upstairs of the old Erie Railroad depot at Piermont, the one-time eastern terminus of the "Weary Erie," at 4:40 A.M. on a September morning in 1915, "five minutes before the day's first train down to Jersey City and 20 minutes before Old Doc Leitner made it up the hill." Kelly's mother, Belle, had been the agent at Piermont since 1908. Five years later, "after a romance conducted in Morse code with the night telegrapher up in Nyack," she married Kelly's father. Although the senior Kelly died several years later, Belle remained an agent and resident of the Piermont depot until 1940. After her retirement from the Erie in 1959, Belle and Tom, her bachelor son, bought the depot from the railroad and once again made it their home. Although his mother died "in the waiting room, at 88" in 1976, Kelly continues to make the depot his home. He has turned "the dim station into an affectionately cluttered museum to railroading and his mom." As Kelly reflected, "This place was always safe. It's so full of memories. And it's all I have really." Unquestionably living in the depot holds special meaning for Tom Kelly, as it surely does for thousands of others who once lived at trackside during the railway age.[30]

THE ALBUM

Early in the twentieth century the Bangor & Aroostock Railroad built several standard two-story depots with living quarters, including ones at Brownville Junction, Glenburn, North Bangor, and Winterport, Maine. The principal reason was surely the lack of suitable local housing. For example, the company constructed the station at Brownville Junction in 1906 to serve a connection with the Canadian Pacific, 4 miles from the village of Brownville. John P. Vander Maas collection.

Built to a standard plan in 1893, the New Limerick, Maine, depot of the Bangor & Aroostock Railroad served a remote village near the border with New Brunswick when this photograph was taken on August 25, 1950. John P. Vander Maas collection.

A Bangor & Aroostock freight train approaches the once-occupied depot at Adams, Maine, on August 21, 1951. Residents used the hand pump in the foreground for their water supply. John P. Vander Maas collection.

The Canadian Pacific Railway, which built across Maine in the late nineteenth century, served some of the state's most isolated countryside, including the hamlet of Chester. Here the company either used an existing dwelling or constructed this farmhouse-style structure, which was vacant when this photograph was taken on September 21, 1957. The Canadian Pacific earlier had covered the building with Insul-brick to save heat (a major concern in this harsh climate) and to reduce overall maintenance. John P. Vander Maas collection.

The agent, perhaps included in this photograph from the early part of the twentieth century, lived in this simple depot owned by the Boston & Maine at Melvin or Melvin's Mills, New Hampshire. Its architectural style could have easily been found on the Nebraska prairie. John P. Vander Maas collection.

West Chelmsford, Massachusetts, situated on
the Boston & Maine's Stoney Brook branch between
Lowell and Ayer, claimed a substantial two-story
depot with living quarters, as seen in this 1928
photograph. John P. Vander Maas collection.

A wonderful illustration of the recyclable nature
of a two-story railroad station with apartment
space is the former Boston & Maine depot at Bethlehem, New Hampshire. Located on a 4-mile stub
line, the B&M served this resort community only
during the summer. Before the railroad abandoned
this appendage, it sold the structure, and the new
owner converted it into a private dwelling. When
this photograph was taken in August 1931, the
building stood unoccupied. Railway & Locomotive
Historical Society collection.

The Boston & Maine's depot at East Kingston, New Hampshire, linked residents of this small farming community on the company's busy Boston-to-Portland line with the outside world. An agent once occupied this spartan structure. John P. Vander Maas collection.

The Old Colony Railroad, a carrier that covered eastern Massachusetts and later joined the New Haven system, consistently built gable-roof, two-story depots with agents' apartments. This turn-of-the-century view of the Matthapoisett structure, complete with Victorian gingerbread and rain barrel, suggests solitude between trains. John P. Vander Maas collection.

The Old Colony Railroad, with its fondness for depots with living quarters, either built or remodeled this two-and-a-half-story stone structure at Avon, Massachusetts, 17 miles from Boston. The building was unquestionably occupied when this photograph was taken on November 24, 1916. Louis W. Goodwin collection.

Although abandoned by the mid-1970s by a successor of the builder, St. Johnsbury & Lake Champaign, the once-occupied depot in the college community of Johnson, Vermont, attests to the logic of providing a dwelling place in this sparsely populated section of the state. John P. Vander Maas collection.

The Housatonic Railroad, the self-proclaimed Berkshire Hills Route and a future component of the New Haven system, built this plain but functional depot at West Cornwall, Connecticut, soon after the Civil War. John P. Vander Maas collection.

This photograph of the Housatonic Railroad's depot at Falls Village, Connecticut, taken on May 13, 1934, reveals the family's laundry and probably its automobile. It also shows the clutter common to stations throughout North America before the demise of passenger and less-than-carload freight service. John P. Vander Maas collection.

Built by either the Central New England & Western Railroad or a successor before the property officially entered the New Haven system in 1927, the depot at Poughkeepsie, New York, served only passengers, but it also likely housed the agent. This photograph dates from the late 1920s. John P. Vander Maas collection.

The Reading Railroad at Linfield, Pennsylvania, on its main line between Philadelphia and Reading, used a former hotel for its depot facility. A predecessor company had remodeled with considerable ease the structure for this purpose. John P. Vander Maas collection.

The longtime Reading Railroad depot at Ogontz, Pennsylvania, is typical of the design and construction styles employed by the North Pennsylvania Railroad during the mid-1870s. This combination depot consists of a single-story unit attached to a two-story agent's dwelling. This station, photographed in 1974, had not served a passenger train since 1899, although it remained a freight agency until the 1940s. John P. Vander Maas collection.

A Reading Railroad predecessor recycled a farmhouse at Mill Lane, Pennsylvania, for a depot, a practice commonly found in areas where railroads followed settlement. John P. Vander Maas collection.

Eventually owned by the Reading system, the former Wilmington & Northern depot at Montchanin, Delaware, reveals a residential-like structure. This photograph dates from July 28, 1974. John P. Vander Maas collection.

The Western Maryland Railway apparently used this antebellum stone house as its depot in Lineboro, Maryland, on its Gettysburg, Pennsylvania, branch. John P. Vander Maas collection.

More a rural cottage than a railroad structure, the Western Maryland's station at McDonogh, Maryland, near Baltimore, was only a flag stop. Most likely the railroad pressed into service an existing house and employed the occupant to be custodian. John P. Vander Maas collection.

The Pennsylvania Railroad suburban depot at Riderwood, Maryland, approximately 8 miles from Baltimore's Calvert Station, contains agent's quarters, as do stations at nearby Cockeysville, Glencoe, Lutherville, Melvale, Mt. Washington, Parkton, and Ruxton. These were built by a predecessor company, Northern Central Railway, from the 1860s to the early 1900s. John P. Vander Maas collection.

One of several suburban stations with living accommodations in the Baltimore area on the Pennsylvania Railroad, the depot at Lutherville, Maryland, about 10 miles from Calvert Station, offers extensive upstairs apartment space. This structure's style of architecture is unusual; few companies selected a New England gambrel roof. John P. Vander Maas collection.

The Philadelphia & Baltimore Central Railroad, later the Philadelphia, Wilmington & Baltimore Railroad and then the Pennsylvania Railroad, used this houselike structure near the campus of Lincoln University, née Ashmun Institute, in Lincoln University, Pennsylvania, 46 miles from Broad Street Station in Philadelphia. Likely built before the Civil War by the college, the depot was remodeled in 1882. It nearly burned down twelve years later and was expanded in 1908 by the addition of a baggage room. John P. Vander Maas collection.

The prosperous Lehigh Valley Railroad erected this specially designed passenger depot with spacious living quarters in South Plainfield, New Jersey, 26 miles from its eastern main line terminus at Jersey City and ferryboat connections to New York City. The presence of commuter trains likely explains why living quarters were included. John P. Vander Maas collection.

A photographer clicked this view of the New York, Susquehanna & Western station at Sussex, New Jersey, on December 26, 1956. Located on the Middletown Division, a 34-mile branch line between Beaver Lake, New Jersey, and Middletown, New York, this depot features a trackside canopy which enhances its appearance and also protects passengers from inclement weather. John P. Vander Maas collection.

In this unidentified scene along the Delaware, Lackawanna & Western Railroad taken in the late nineteenth century, a train crew gathers with possibly the children of the local agent. Because the DL&W traversed isolated sections of Pennsylvania's anthracite coal region, it erected some depots with apartments. Railway & Locomotive Historical Society collection.

Life began in 1899 for the 13-mile Chestnut Ridge Railway. On its 11-mile main line from Palmerton, Pennsylvania, to Kunkleton, Pennsylvania, it served the hamlet of Little Gap, 7 miles from Palmerton. This 1951 photograph shows what was surely a former house converted into a railway facility. The agent/custodian occupied part of the first floor and all of the second. John P. Vander Maas collection.

The Lehigh Valley Transit Company, a larger and much more vigorous operation than the Chestnut Ridge Railway, operated electric interurban service between the Pennsylvania cities of Allentown, Bethlehem, and Philadelphia. Like many steam short lines and "juice" roads, the company used former houses for depots. This view shows the station at Hatfield on November 24, 1950, a year before the firm abandoned operations. John P. Vander Maas collection.

Few railroads in the South opted for two-story depots with living quarters. One that did with some frequency was the Chesapeake & Ohio Railway. Its depot at Glade, West Virginia, seen in this August 1935 photograph, gave residents reasonably good accommodations. Certainly they lived more comfortably than did track laborers who stayed in company bunkcars by the station. John P. Vander Maas collection.

Lambs, Michigan, located on the 34-mile Port Huron–Almont branch of the Pere Marquette Railroad, was a hamlet with limited housing, so the company provided an apartment. The unusually large windows on the end elevation of this cheaply built depot indicate that it may have served another community function, such as post office and general store. Railroads occasionally rented out space for such purposes. John P. Vander Maas collection.

The Duluth, South Shore & Atlantic decided that Paynesville, Michigan, situated in a remote section of the Upper Peninsula, needed housing for its agent. Rare for depots of the general region, this one is made of manufactured block, probably locally produced. While more expensive than wood, these blocks made for a warmer building with less exterior upkeep. A Western Union sign by the waiting-room door announces telegraphic service to the world. John P. Vander Maas collection.

The Milwaukee Road, one of several trunk roads which served Michigan's Upper Peninsula, erected this 24' x 60' depot with living quarters in the hamlet of Rockland on its McKeever-Ontonagon branch shortly after 1900. John P. Vander Maas collection.

The Milwaukee Road agent who lived in Browntown, Wisconsin, on the company's Mineral Point Division in the southwestern section of the state, resided in an inexpensively built board-and-batten structure of standard design. The employee endured a cramped apartment with limited natural light, as indicated by the three trackside "eyebrow" windows. John P. Vander Maas collection.

Used by both the Milwaukee Road and the Illinois Central, this standard-type depot at Dill, Wisconsin, resembles the one at Browntown, Wisconsin, except that it is larger with additional space for the agent's quarters. John P. Vander Maas collection.

Two rival Granger roads, Chicago & North Western and Chicago, Milwaukee & St. Paul, shared a facility in Grand Crossing, Wisconsin, near La Crosse. This scene from the turn of the century suggests a mid-western farmhouse rather than a station building. *John P. Vander Maas collection.*

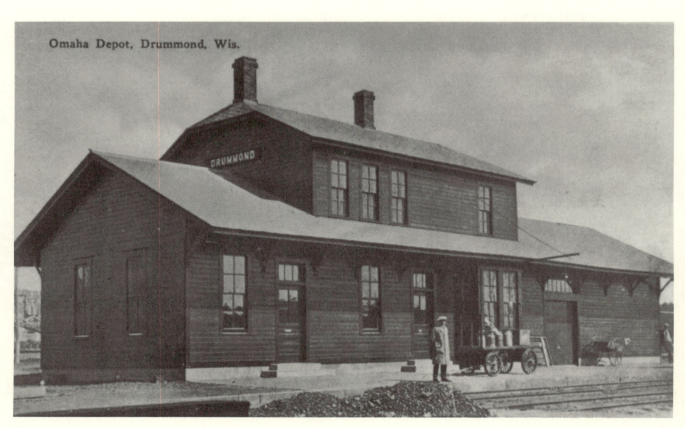

Omaha Depot, Drummond, Wis.

The Chicago, St. Paul, Minneapolis & Omaha Railway, better known as the Omaha Road and long controlled by the Chicago & North Western Railway, erected this two-story depot at Drummond, Wisconsin, probably in the nineteenth century. The pile of coal in the foreground may have spilled accidentally or been dumped intentionally for use by the agent in stoves for heating both the depot's public and private areas. John P. Vander Maas collection.

Much more representative of some depots in
the East, the Chicago & North Western's station in
Kaukauna, Wisconsin, probably a former residence, likely accommodated the local agent. John P.
Vander Maas collection.

A local freight train rolls into the Plainview, Minnesota, station of the Chicago & North Western Railway about 1890. This cheaply built wooden depot at the end of the 16-mile "Plainview Railroad Branch" in southeastern Minnesota contains only a modest second-floor apartment. Author's collection.

Occasionally Granger roads, for example the Rock Island, used store buildings with living space for depots. In the crossroads village of Bayfield, Iowa, a station 8 miles west of Muscatine, such a structure met the company's needs. Likely the Rock Island paid the storekeeper to be custodian. *John P. Vander Maas collection.*

When the Iowa Central Railroad built its two-story depot at Fremont, Iowa, in the 1880s, it selected a favorite design for the region's residential dwellings, the "I-house," named because of its popularity in Iowa, Illinois, and Indiana. A one-room-deep floor plan and a front portico characterize this structure. *John P. Vander Maas collection.*

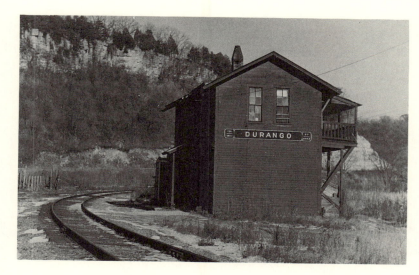

Either the Chicago Great Western or a predecessor, the Minnesota & Northwestern or the Chicago, St. Paul & Kansas City, constructed an unusual two-story depot at Durango, Iowa, in a rugged section of the state. To enhance privacy and to capture summer breezes, a combination stairway and porch face away from trackside. John P. Vander Maas collection.

The Winona & Southwestern, later part of the Chicago Great Western, built several two-story depots with living quarters along its lines in northern Iowa and southern Minnesota during the early 1890s, including this one at Little Cedar, Iowa. The design likely was copied from the Burlington, Cedar Rapids & Northern, which also served the region. John P. Vander Maas collection.

The Soo Line built hundreds of its Second Class depots throughout its system, including ones at Palisade, Minnesota, on its Moose Lake–Thief River Falls line and at Whitetail, Montana, the end of its Whitetail branch. John P. Vander Maas collection.

The classic profile of a Soo Line Second Class depot is seen in this April 1974 photograph of the station at Rolette, North Dakota, built in 1905. The United States Railroad Administration, which controlled the nation's carriers during World War I, ordered the building relocated in 1918 to house a money-saving joint agency with the Great Northern. The lengthened freight room reflects the need for additional space to handle the increased business at this rail junction. Author's collection.

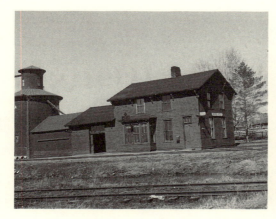

A *predecessor of the Minneapolis & St. Louis Railway, the Wisconsin, Minnesota & Pacific, which constructed 123 miles of line between Morton, Minnesota, and Watertown, South Dakota, in 1883 and 1884, opted almost exclusively for depots with agents' apartments. Examples include the structures at Boyd, Clarkfield, and Wood Lake, Minnesota. Once painted a snappy Kelly green, these depots, although often still occupied, became shabby during the twilight of small-town agency service. John P. Vander Maas collection.*

Train-time is about to occur at the Rock Island station in South English, Iowa, during the summer of 1912. A 4-4-0 type locomotive, an American Standard, is steaming up to the platform. This depot, originally built by the Burlington, Cedar Rapids & Northern, a Rock Island predecessor, was a style that served several dozen communities in Iowa, Minnesota, and South Dakota. John P. Vander Maas collection.

In the depots at Clermont, Greene, Hardy, Marble Rock, Maynard, Plato, and West Branch, Iowa, the Burlington, Cedar Rapids & Northern showed a passion for this style of two-story depot with agent's apartment. Variations occurred between the 1870s and 1902, the year the company officially entered the fold of the Rock Island. Most shared that "cookie-cutter" look. The employment of large roof-support brackets with the pronounced roof overhang made these structures rather striking and more attractive than most used by such competitors as the Chicago & North Western and the Milwaukee Road. John P. Vander Maas collection.

A *wholly owned affiliate of the Rock Island, the Chicago, Kansas & Nebraska Railway built dozens of unusually large frame depots in Nebraska and especially Kansas in 1886 and 1887. These distinctive structures sported a first-story awning and a roof line broken by a prominent window dormer and hipped angles. The depots at Alta Vista and Hoyt, Kansas, are typical, while the one at Bucklin, Kansas (rear view), a more important station and junction point, is a variation. John P. Vander Maas collection.*

The Milwaukee Road built its attractive 24' x 60' depots in the western Iowa communities of Lytton and Nemaha early in the century. Both may have been replacement structures. John P. Vander Maas collection.

The engineering department at the Milwaukee Road showed a keen interest in two-story depots with agent's quarters and used several standard plans. The company was always willing to make modifications, as revealed in the unusually long freight house on its depot at Hettinger, North Dakota. The normal lengths can be seen at Jamaica, Iowa, and Lucerne, Missouri. Some of the architectural detail, though stylish at the time of construction, disappeared over the decades; the photograph of the Jamaica depot dates from 1907, the one at Lucerne from 1957. John P. Vander Maas collection.

While the phenomenon of building station hotels appeared largely in the East and before the 1880s, exceptions occurred. When the Chicago & North Western entered a remote area of the southern Iowa coalfields early in the century, it needed both a depot and a hotel at its terminal in the unincorporated settlement of Miami in Monroe County. Suitable living space was so scarce that the railroad also erected a house for its section foreman. John P. Vander Maas collection.

The Toledo & North Western, which the Chicago & North Western controlled, liked two-story depots with agent's quarters along its 243-mile main stem between the Iowa communities of Tama and Hawarden and also along its branches. Most came from either No. 1 or No. 2 plans. The former (Alden and Lawn Hill) had three upstairs windows overlooking trackside and a long freight room. The latter (Hubbard and Kamrar), however, had four of these second-floor windows but a short freight house. The No. 1 measured 22' x 72' and the No. 2 22' x 56'—the variable was the length of the freight section. John P. Vander Maas collection.

Numerous stations along the Fremont, Elkhorn & Missouri Valley Railroad (FE&MV), part of the Chicago & North Western system, received depots like those at Battle Creek and Stuart, Nebraska. Similar in style, they nevertheless represent variations. The company added an unusually long freight house at Stuart, attesting to the expandability of this type of combination plan. The FE&MV, which initially served large sections of empty prairie in northern Nebraska, also built one-story depots with apartment space. John P. Vander Maas collection.

The Chicago & North Western erected numerous two-story depots of board-and-batten construction, such as the one in Centerville, South Dakota. Wishing to minimize costs, the company ordered its carpenters to nail boards on a building's framing with the cracks battened, but this method did not create a warm, comfortable structure in cold weather. John P. Vander Maas collection.

The agent at Underwood, South Dakota, wearing his required uniform and cap, poses by the recently completed standard two-story Chicago & North Western depot about 1910. To break the monotony of this design, the company added an extended bay section on the office and attached two roof finials. John P. Vander Maas collection.

Although the Chicago & North Western line opened forty-seven years before this photograph was taken, Wall, South Dakota, remained a small community with limited housing. The structure behind the standard depot is a standard section house, often used in the state's West River Country. John P. Vander Maas collection.

The two-story standard Chicago & North Western depot at Midland, South Dakota, 81 miles east of Wall, was built by its affiliate, Pierre, Rapid City & Northwestern. It is a fine example of the wooden combination depots constructed by prairie roads; they were nearly always devoid of decorative features. The structure eventually became the focal point of a community museum. John P. Vander Maas collection.

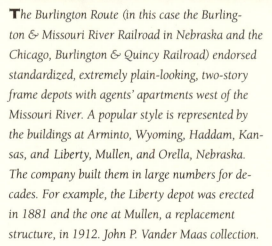

*T*he Burlington Route (in this case the Burlington & Missouri River Railroad in Nebraska and the Chicago, Burlington & Quincy Railroad) endorsed standardized, extremely plain-looking, two-story frame depots with agents' apartments west of the Missouri River. A popular style is represented by the buildings at Arminto, Wyoming, Haddam, Kansas, and Liberty, Mullen, and Orella, Nebraska. The company built them in large numbers for decades. For example, the Liberty depot was erected in 1881 and the one at Mullen, a replacement structure, in 1912. John P. Vander Maas collection.

The Burlington Route varied somewhat the appearance of its ubiquitous two-story frame depots west of the Missouri River, as seen in the 1903 view of the depot at Ericson, Nebraska (with its residents), and the 1955 one of Grover, Colorado. John P. Vander Maas collection.

The Colorado Limited awaits a highball at the Burlington Route depot at Akron, Colorado, in 1910. The ladder on the side of the building, a common feature on such frame structures, is for a fire emergency and for use in making repairs. John P. Vander Maas collection.

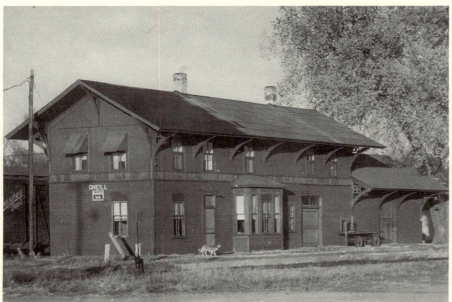

The Burlington Route, like other carriers that emerged out of the process of system building, inherited depot types from predecessor and acquired roads. In this case the Burlington got two-story structures with living quarters (which it gladly accepted) built by the Pacific Short Line, officially the Nebraska & Western Railroad, a carrier that constructed a 129-mile line between Sioux City, Iowa, and O'Neill, Nebraska, between 1889 and 1890. The Pacific Short Line subsequently came under the control of the Great Northern Railway, and that company sold it to the Burlington in 1908. Examples of these Pacific Short Line structures are found at Brunswick and O'Neill, Nebraska, the latter a larger version completed on August 7, 1890. John P. Vander Maas collection.

When the Missouri Pacific, under the generalship of Jay Gould, commonly known as "the most hated man in America," pushed westward through Kansas toward Pueblo, Colorado, in 1887, it built mostly single-story combination depots with hip roofs but without apartments. An exception occurred at Comiskey, Kansas. The company believed that this village required living quarters. Yet, the Missouri Pacific remained committed to its favorite roof style. John P. Vander Maas collection.

MoP Depot   Comiskey, Kansas

The Santa Fe needed housing for its agent in Wakarusa, Kansas, so it constructed this two-story depot of standard design. The railroad built only a few of these structures in the state but erected many more further west where housing shortages were common. John P. Vander Maas collection.

This 20' x 40' two-story Santa Fe depot at Anthony, formerly La Tuna, Texas, once served the community of Las Cruces, New Mexico, but was moved to the townsite early in the century to replace two portable 8' x 28' car bodies. In 1967, four years after this photograph, the Santa Fe remodeled this structure into a single-story one, a fate that occurred to scores of depots that once provided upstairs housing. John P. Vander Maas collection.

The Rock Island selected a two-story depot for Asher, Oklahoma, the end of its 27-mile Tecumseh branch. Seemingly, this photograph, taken on March 14, 1942, indicates that the apartment had been vacated, and soon would the line itself. John P. Vander Maas collection.

The Cassville & Exeter, originally the Cassville & Western, a 5-mile short line in the Ozarks of Missouri, began operations in 1896 as a steam road but in 1911 became electrified and then returned to steam power. Later it operated with a diesel locomotive. The road's modest two-story depot at Cassville appears in this November 29, 1953, photograph, three years before the company folded. John P. Vander Maas collection.

Narrow-gauge railroads might select two-story depots with living space. The 162-mile Rio Grande Southern Railroad, which principally served four mining camps (Placerville, Ophir, Rico, and Telluride) in southwestern Colorado, constructed such a structure at Ophir in the early 1890s, as seen in this May 30, 1947, photograph taken five years before this slim-width road ended operations. John P. Vander Maas collection.

Atlantic Canada, too, saw construction of two-story depots with living quarters. This area resembled northern New England by lacking adequate local housing. This photograph, taken on April 25, 1954, shows the station of the Dominion Atlantic Railway, Land of Evangeline Route, at Brooklyn, Nova Scotia. John P. Vander Maas collection.

The Intercolonial Railway, eventually part of the Canadian National, created an attractive homelike depot for its station at Oxford, Nova Scotia, at the turn of the century. Unlike structures that dominated the Canadian West, some in the East were of brick and occasionally stone. The Intercolonial also employed wooden construction. The remarkably ornate depot at River John, Nova Scotia, with its four gabled dormers, is an example. John P. Vander Maas collection.

Located 121 miles north of Montreal, the Canadian National station at Ste. Thecle, Quebec, was designed by a predecessor road, the Canadian Northern Quebec Railway, early in the century. When these children performed for a photographer in the summer of 1963, the Canadian National continued to staff the agency with a live-in employee. John P. Vander Maas collection.

The Third Class Canadian Northern depot at Minto, Manitoba, constructed in 1906, sports an amazingly long addition to its central core. This photograph was taken in 1968, near the end of this then Canadian National–owned structure. John P. Vander Maas collection.

The Canadian Northern Type C design was used at Vavenby, British Columbia, in 1915, and cost approximately $2,700. More than thirty structures of this type appeared in the province, including the one at Tranquille built in 1916. John P. Vander Maas collection. The floor plan is for the Vavenby depot. Author's collection.

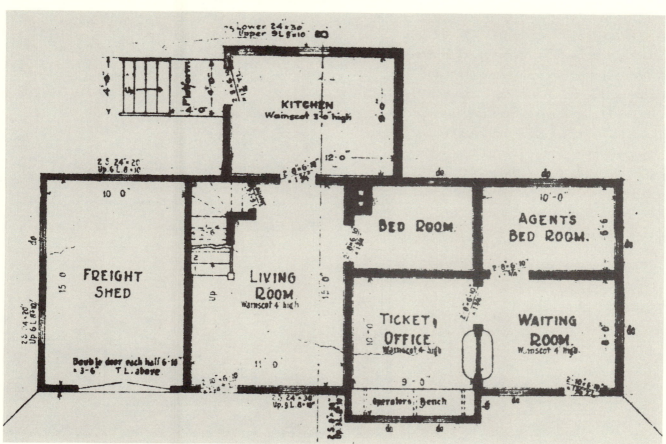

Before its nationalization in 1920, the Grand
Trunk Pacific enthusiastically embraced standard
depot structures with living quarters. By far the
road's most popular design was its Type E; the company erected more than two hundred of these distinctive buildings with their bellcast roofs between
1910 and 1916, including ones in the Alberta villages of Elnora in 1911 and Bashaw in 1913. The
cozy apartment includes a 15' x 10'6" living room
and an attached 14'6" x 12' kitchen on the first
floor and two 15' x 15'7" bedrooms on the second
floor. John P. Vander Maas collection.

Located on the Canadian Pacific's Trans-Continental Route, the depot at Indian Head, Saskatchewan, is seen early in the century. The station has apparently attracted travelers and on-lookers, including Native Americans and perhaps the agent and his dog. The simplicity of this carbon-copy architectural style is evident. Railway & Locomotive Historical Society collection.

The depot at Carstairs, Alberta, represents an early standard Canadian Pacific design used in the West. This side view reveals the 10' x 12' kitchen annex. The isolated village was located on the company's Calgary-to-Edmonton line. John P. Vander Maas collection.

Typical of the more sophisticated two-story plans used by Canadian roads, the Canadian Pacific depot at Kandahar, Saskatchewan, with its gabled dormer, is one of nearly two hundred of this type. John P. Vander Maas collection.

This August 1963 view of the depot at Warner, Alberta, shows a popular standard two-story style built by the Canadian Pacific in western Canada between 1907 and World War I. Milk cans await a passenger or mixed train. John P. Vander Maas collection.

Situated 10 miles from Calgary on the Canadian Pacific's Calgary-to-Lethbridge line, the Midnapore, Alberta, depot, similar to the one at Warner, Alberta, attracts a small crowd at train-time. John P. Vander Maas collection.

The Canadian Pacific developed this standard
design early in the century and used it for its
depot at Moyie, British Columbia, in the
southeastern part of the province. This building features interesting lines, highlighted by a
second-story mansard roof. John P. Vander
Maas collection.

After experimenting with several standard designs early in the century, the Canadian Pacific adopted the one seen in this 1968 photograph of the depot at Asquith, Saskatchewan. A second story topped by a low pyramid roof and broken by a hip dormer with two windows characterizes this style. The Canadian Pacific duplicated this plan more than forty times in the province. *John P. Vander Maas collection.*

The Northern Pacific, the first of the northern transcontinentals, frequently opted for this standard two-story style along its far-flung system from Minnesota to Washington, including the station at Wilbur, Washington. *John P. Vander Maas collection.*

Reardan, Washington, located on the Washington Central branch of the Northern Pacific 42 miles from Spokane, got this roomy two-story depot about 1900. In its final years of service, the Northern Pacific did little maintenance work; the lack of painting attests to this inattention. *John P. Vander Maas collection.*

The Northern Pacific picked a standard two-story plan for its station at Wibaux, Montana, in ranch country near the North Dakota border and on its transcontinental route. John P. Vander Maas collection.

N.P. PASSENGER STATION.   WIBAUX, MONT.

The Oregon River & Navigation Company, later part of the Union Pacific system, showed considerable flair with its design for a two-story depot with living quarters at its Dayton, Washington, station. This photograph was taken in September 1955. John P. Vander Maas collection.

The Oregon River & Navigation Company's depot at Wallula, Washington, illustrates a design this road selected repeatedly for stations in the Pacific Northwest. The agent likely inhabited the building when this photograph was taken on May 5, 1941. John P. Vander Maas collection.

The Oregon Short Line, an affiliate of the
Union Pacific, built depots like the ones at Downey
and Richfield, Idaho, at several locations. Roof-
support brackets and gable bargeboards provide
modest and inexpensive decoration to an otherwise
plain structure. John P. Vander Maas collection.

The Oregon Short Line, faced with the need for
depots at numerous stations, opted for this standard-type plan at Armstead, Montana. The building's hip roof, including the one over the office and
dwelling sections, creates a positive visual effect.
John P. Vander Maas collection.

SOU. PAC. DEPOT
BRENTWOOD, CAL.

S P DEPOT
LOVELOCK, NEV.

The Southern Pacific Railroad erected more than
a dozen two-story depots with living quarters like
those found at Brentwood, California, and Lovelock, Nevada, mostly during the 1870s. These
Stick-style affairs predate another popular version,
the Benicia type. John P. Vander Maas collection.

SOU. PAC. DEPOT
DANVILLE, CALIF.

A *photographer snapped this image of the Benicia-
type depot at Danville, California, on the Southern
Pacific's Avon-Livermore branch on October 10,
1940. The agent added window boxes, which
showed the pride some families exhibited toward
their trackside homes. John P. Vander Maas
collection.*

While Texas boasted many more single-story depots without apartments than it did two-story ones with them, the West Texas community of Marathon could claim the latter. This version of the Southern Pacific's popular Standard No. 22 plan still served the railroad's needs in August 1971, although it likely no longer housed the agent. John P. Vander Maas collection.

As with other carriers, the Burlington Route remodeled dozens of depots after World War II. Some two-story ones became smaller, one-story affairs. With access to automobiles and all-weather roads, agents no longer required apartments. The demise of the passenger train meant that waiting rooms were also superfluous. Yet the railroad still sought office space for the agent and storage for less-than-carload and express shipments. Although the Burlington did not radically change its depot at Guernsey, Wyoming, it added an exterior covering, installed insulation, and likely altered the freight room. John P. Vander Maas collection.

Situated at the end of the Milwaukee Road's 5-mile Belgrade stub in western Montana, the two-story Belgrade depot stands abandoned in 1960, the fate of many similar structures by this time. John P. Vander Maas collection.

The Soo Line Standard Second Class depot at Mylo, North Dakota, built in 1905, is nearly a memory by spring 1974. Author's collection.

NOTES

THE RAILROAD AND THE DEPOT

1. *"Appendix" to Second Report of the Directors of the New-York and Erie Railroad Company, to the Stockholders* (New York: Egbert Hedge, 1841), p. 8; Edward Hungerford, *Men of Erie: A Story of Human Effort* (New York: Random House, 1946), pp. 53–54; Edward Harold Mott, *Between the Ocean and the Lakes: The Story of Erie* (New York: John S. Collins, 1899), pp. 323–24.

2. *"Appendix" to Second Report,* p. 8; George W. Hilton, *American Narrow Gauge Railroads* (Stanford, Calif.: Stanford University Press, 1990), pp. 31, 36.

3. See Hilton, *American Narrow Gauge Railroads.*

4. Albro Martin, *Railroads Triumphant: The Growth, Rejection & Rebirth of a Vital American Force* (New York: Oxford University Press, 1992), pp. 12–17; *Erie Railroad Magazine* 54 (May 1958): 14.

5. John F. Stover, *History of the Baltimore and Ohio Railroad* (West Lafayette, Ind.: Purdue University Press, 1987), pp. 30–34; Herbert H. Harwood, Jr., "History Where You Don't Expect It: Some Surprising Survivors," *Railroad History* 166 (Spring 1992): 104–07.

6. Interview with Louis W. Goodwin, Northfield, Connecticut, May 16, 1992. A New Haven engineer related the Merwinsville story to Goodwin. Another version appears in B. A. Botkin and Alvin F. Harlow, *A Treasury of Railroad Folklore* (New York: Crown Publishers, 1953), p. 177, and it parallels the one repeated by the Merwinsville Hotel Restoration Association.

7. "The Oldest Railroad Station," *Maine Central Messenger* 11 (February–March 1975): 6–8; Herbert H. Harwood, Jr., "Two Stations Which Weren't," *The Bulletin: Railroad Station Historical Society* 5 (November–December 1972): 72–73; W. P. Beesley to author, January 14, 1977.

8. "Apartments in Railway Service Buildings," *Electric Railway Journal* 42 (August 30, 1913): 3.

9. Ron Brown, *The Train Doesn't Stop Here Any More: An Illustrated History of Railway Stations in Canada* (Peterborough, Ontario: Broadview Press, 1991), p. 127; John A. Droege, *Passenger Terminals and Trains* (New York: McGraw-Hill, 1916), p. 268.

10. See "Breaking In: A Study for the Adaptive Reuse of Three County Jail/Sheriff's Residence Buildings," Ohio Historic Preservation Office and others, Columbus, Ohio, 1991.

11. Walter G. Berg, *Buildings and Structures of American Railroads: A Reference Work* (New York: John Wiley & Sons, 1904), p. 246; Droege, *Passenger Terminals and Trains*, p. 259.

12. Dianne Newell, "The Short-lived Phenomenon of Railroad Station-Hotels," *Historic Preservation* (July–September 1974): 31–36; Francis D. Donovan, "Railroad Station-Hotels of the Nineteenth Century," *The Bulletin: Railroad Station Historical Society* 16 (November–December 1983): 81–83.

13. Lucius Beebe, *Mixed Train Daily: A Book of Short-Line Railroads* (1947; rpt., Berkeley, Calif.: Howell-North, 1961), p. 25; Allen W. Trelease, *The North Carolina Railroad, 1849–1871 and the Modernization of North Carolina* (Chapel Hill: University of North Carolina Press, 1991), pp. 327–46.

14. Berg, *Buildings and Structures of American Railroads*, pp. 258–60; John F. Gilbert, ed., *Crossties to the Depot* (Raleigh, N.C.: Crossties Press, 1982), vol. 1, *Virginia Railroad Stations*, pp. 36–37, 39.

15. "Standard Plans for Small Stations: West Shore Railroad," *Engineering News* 19 (March 31, 1888): 246; "Standard Stations—West Shore Railroad," *The Bulletin: Railroad Station Historical Society* 19 (November–December 1986): 95.

16. Henry A. Harter, *Fairy Tale Railroad* (Sylvan Beach, N.Y.: North Country Books, 1979), pp. 61, 174–75, 178, 189–91; Edward A. Lewis, *New England Country Depots* (Arcade, N.Y.: Baggage Car, 1973), pp. 12–13, 18, 28, 35–36, 40, 86, 89, 91; Robert F. Lord, *Downeast Depots: Maine Railroad Stations in the Steam Era* (Collinsville, Conn.: privately printed, 1986), pp. 10–12, 14–16, 18, 20–23, 26–27, 51; Louis W. Goodwin to author, September 24, 1991; James R. McFarland to author, October 31, 1991, hereafter cited as McFarland letter.

17. Robert F. Lord to author, August 28, 1991; McFarland letter.

18. Louis W. Goodwin to author, August 31, 1991.

19. Wilson E. Jones, ed., *The Next Station Will Be . . . An Album of Photographs of Railroad Depots in 1910*, vol. 3 (Livingston, N.J.: Railroadians of America, 1975), pp. 9–10, 17, 22, 39–41; "Long Island Railroad Stations," *The Bulletin: Railroad Station Historical Society* 19 (September–October 1986): 72–73.

20. Berg, *Buildings and Structures of American Railroads*, p. 294.

21. Herbert H. Harwood, Jr., to author, January 21, 1992; Herbert H. Harwood, Jr., *Philadelphia's Victorian Suburban Stations* (Crete, Neb.: Railway History Monograph, 1975), pp. 1–2, 6, 33–34.

22. Harwood, *Suburban Stations*, pp. 4, 37–42; "The Designing of Small Railway Stations," *American Architect* 100 (October 4, 1911): 130.

23. H. Roger Grant, "Depot: Economy and Style at Trackside," *Timeline* 1 (October 1984): 59; Ira J. Bach and Susan Wolfson, *A Guide to Chicago's Train Stations Past and Present* (Athens: Ohio University Press, 1986), pp. 44–45, 56–57, 66–69, 106–09, 128–29, 132–35, 144–45, 188–89; Wilson E. Jones, ed., *The Next Station Will Be . . . An Album of Photographs of Railroad Depots in 1910*, vol. 10. (Livingston, N.J.: Railroadians of America, 1988), p. 56.

24. Larry E. Easton, "Wisconsin Central's 1898 Combination Depot," *The Soo* 11 (January 1989): 26–49.

25. Robert C. Brown to author, December 12, 1991, hereafter cited as Brown letter; H. Roger Grant and Charles W. Bohi, *The Country Railroad Station in America*, rev. ed. (Sioux Falls, S.D.: Center for Western Studies, 1988), pp. 85–88.

26. Lewis Atherton, *Main Street on the Middle Border* (Bloomington: Indiana University Press, 1954), pp. 222–29.

27. Fred W. Peterson, *Homes in the Heartland: Balloon Frame Farmhouses of the Upper Midwest, 1850–1920* (Lawrence: University Press of Kansas, 1992), pp. 24, 26–30; Arthur M. Hart, "M. A. Disbrow & Company: Catalogue Architecture," *Palimpsest* 56 (July–August 1975): 98–119; Daniel J. Boorstin, *The Americans: The National Experience* (New York: Random House, 1965), pp. 148–52; Hamlin Garland, *A Son of the Middle Border* (1917; rpt., New York: Macmillan, 1962), p. 312; John MacMaster to Charles W. Perkins, September 2, 1894, Chicago, Burlington & Quincy Papers, Newberry Library, Chicago, hereafter cited as CB&Q Papers.

28. Droege, *Passenger Terminals and Trains*, p. 264.

29. Quoted in letter from William Armstrong to author, December 14, 1976.

30. George W. Holdrege to Charles W. Perkins, n.d., CB&Q Papers.

31. Robert E. Pounds, *Santa Fe Depots: The Western Lines* (Dallas: Kachina Press, 1984), p. 22. The La Tuna depot exemplifies the versatility of a standard combination design. The Santa Fe added on to the freight room at the time of the building's removal from Las Cruces, New Mexico, and rebuilt it in 1967 as a single-story 24′ × 30′ structure. See Pounds, *Santa Fe Depots*, p. 73.

32. Charles W. Bohi and H. Roger Grant, "The Country Railroad Station as Corporate Logo," *Pioneer America* 11 (August 1979): 117–29; Frank E. Vyzralek, H. Roger Grant, and Charles Bohi, "North Dakota's Railroad Depots: Standardization on the Soo Line," *North Dakota History* 42 (Winter 1975): 9.

33. Vyzralek, Grant, and Bohi, "North Dakota's Railroad Depots," pp. 8, 13.

34. Ibid., pp. 8, 15, 25.

35. Charles W. Bohi and H. Roger Grant, "The Standardized Railroad Station in Saskatchewan: The Case of the Canadian National System," *Saskatchewan History* 29 (Autumn 1976): 81, 89; Charles W. Bohi and H. Roger Grant, "The Country Railroad Station of Manitoba," *Manitoba Pageant* 23 (Spring 1978): 8–11.

36. Charles W. Bohi, *Canadian National's Western Depots: The Country Stations in Western Canada* (Toronto: Railfare Enterprises, 1977), p. 110.

37. Ibid., p. 121; Charles W. Bohi, "Canadian National Third Class Depots," *The Bulletin: Railroad Station Historical Society* 16 (January–February 1983): 1–5.

38. R. M. Brown to author, February 28, 1977.

39. Edwin D. Culp, *Stations West* (Caldwell, Idaho: Caxton Printers, 1972), pp. 50–51, 54–55, 62; Thornton Waite, *Eastern Idaho Railroad Stations* (Crete, Neb.: Railroad Station Historical Society, 1978), pp. 19, 31.

40. Jeff S. Asay, "Wasco, Oregon, Depot," *The Bulletin: Railroad Station Historical Society* 16 (March–April, 1983): 15, 17.

41. Keith L. Bryant, Jr., *History of the Atchison, Topeka and Santa Fe Railway* (New York: Macmillan, 1974), pp. 192–94; "Santa Fe Standard Concrete Depots," *Railway Age* 41 (March 23, 1906): 439; Pounds, *Santa Fe Depots*, pp. 8, 176–80.

42. Pounds, *Santa Fe Depots*, pp. 176–77; Karen J. Weitze, *California's Mission Revival* (Los Angeles: Hennessey & Ingalls, 1984), pp. 84–88; "Santa Fe Standard Concrete Depots," p. 438. Another Santa Fe affiliate, the San Francisco & San Joaquin Valley Railway, embraced somewhat similar designs in the mid-1890s along its newly constructed 250-mile route between the California communities of Stockton and Bakersfield. See *Engineering News and American Railway Journal* 36 (October 29, 1896): 274, 281.

43. Henry E. Bender, Jr., "Standard-Design Depots," manuscript in possession of author.

44. Ibid.; Harold A. Edmonson, ed., *Railroad Station Planbook* (Milwaukee: Kalmbach Books, 1977), pp. 33–39; Gary B. Coombs, *Goleta Depot: The History of a Rural Railroad Station* (Goleta, Calif.: Institute for American Research, 1982), p. 16; interview with Lynn Farrar, Detroit, Michigan, September 27, 1991, hereafter cited as Farrar interview; interview with Arthur L. Lloyd, Detroit, Michigan, September 27, 1991.

45. Bach and Wolfson, *Chicago's Train Stations*, pp. 70–71; Grant and Bohi, *The Country Railroad Station*, p. 139; R. M. Brown to author, January 20, 1977.

46. Berg, *Buildings and Structures of American Railroads*, pp. 14, 23.

47. George H. Gibson, "High-Speed Electric Interurban Railways," *Annual Report of the Board of Regents of the Smithsonian Institution* (Washington, D.C., 1904), p. 311; George W. Hilton and John F. Due, *The Electric Interurban Railways in America* (Stanford, Calif.: Stanford University Press, 1960), pp. 186, 381–82, 389.

48. Grant and Bohi, *The Country Railroad Station*, pp. 177, 185; Clifford A. Elliott, "Home Attractions Keep Track Laborers Satisfied," *Electric Railway Journal* 52 (July 27, 1918): 150.

49. *Electric Railway Journal* (September 27, 1913): 500; Francis H. Parker, *Indiana Railroad Depots: A Threatened Heritage* (Muncie, Ind.: Ball State University Department of Urban Planning, 1989), pp. 34, 43.

The Agent and the Depot

1. H. Roger Grant, ed., *Brownie the Boomer: The Life of Charles P. Brown, an American Railroader* (DeKalb: Northern Illinois University Press, 1991), pp. 97–98.

2. "The Autobiography of Dan Knight," pp. 256, 260, manuscript in possession of author.

3. Quinten L. Farmen to author, February 4, 1978, hereafter cited as Farmen letter.

4. Lloyd Reeves to author, February 26, 1992, hereafter cited as Lloyd Reeves letter; Brown letter; R. Dale Reeves to author, May 6, 1992, hereafter cited as Dale Reeves letter.

5. Dan Knight to author, October 5, 1982; Dale Reeves letter.

6. "Autobiography of C. C. Searls," pp. 4–5, manuscript in possession of author, hereafter cited as Searls autobiography.

7. Vyzralek, Grant, and Bohi, "North Dakota's Railroad Depots," p. 16; G. A. Holmes memorandum, February 1, 1926, in possession of author; Brown, *The Train Doesn't Stop Here Any More*, p. 129.

8. Michael M. Bartels to author, January 31, 1992; *Daily Huronite* (Huron, S.D.), January 8, 1950; Coombs, *Goleta Depot*, pp. 44–45. Noise might possess a positive dimension. The daughter of a Southern Pacific agent at Goleta, California, considered the passing of a train to have an advantage. As a teenager returning home late after a date "and wishing to avoid parental interrogation, she would simply wait for the next train to pass. Its noise would kindly mask her footfalls as she stole up the hollow wooden stairs to the safety of her room." Coombs, *Goleta Depot*, pp. 39–40.

9. Brown, *The Train Doesn't Stop Here Any More*, p. 129; Vyzralek, Grant, and Bohi, "North Dakota's Railroad Depots," p. 15.

10. Coombs, *Goleta Depot*, p. 45; Farmen letter.

11. Brown, *The Train Doesn't Stop Here Any More*, p. 129.

12. Ibid., p. 133.

13. Brown letter; H. Roger Grant, "The Railroad Station Agent in Small-Town Iowa," *Palimpsest* 64 (May–June 1983): 102; Searls autobiography, p. 4.

14. *Daily Huronite*, January 8, 1950.

15. John C. Hudson, *Plains Country Towns* (Minneapolis: University of Minnesota Press, 1985), p. 90.

16. Grant, "The Railroad Station Agent in Small-Town Iowa," p. 94.

17. Ibid.; *Des Moines Register*, April 20, 1975.

18. Brown letter; unidentified newspaper clipping in possession of author; Reeves letter; Elizabeth A. Willmont, *Meet Me at the Station* (Toronto: Gage Publishing, 1976), p. 30.

19. Quinten L. Farmen to author, May 9, 1978; H. A. Stimson, *Depot Days* (Lake Worth, Fla.: privately printed, 1972), p. 7.

20. *Western Guard* (Madison, Minn.), December 24, 1970.

21. Dan Knight to author, September 26, 1979, hereafter cited as Knight letter.

22. Farrar interview; Lloyd Reeves letter; Dale Reeves letter.

23. Stimson, *Depot Days*, p. 10.

24. Ibid.

25. Kenneth R. Garwick, "Those Were the Days," *Good Old Days* 16 (January 1980): 3–5, 54.

26. Knight letter.

27. Ibid.

28. *Daily Plainsman* (Huron, S.D.), February 10, 1957.

29. James L. Ehernberger and Francis G. Gschwind, "The Vanishing Railroad Station," *The Bulletin: Railroad Station Historical Society* 3 (May–June 1970): 19–21.

30. *New York Times*, April 19, 1991.

SELECTED BIBLIOGRAPHY

Alexander, Edwin P. *Down at the Depot: American Railroad Stations from 1831 to 1920.* New York: Bramhill House, 1970.

Bach, Ira J., and Susan Wolfson. *A Guide to Chicago's Train Stations Past and Present.* Athens: Ohio University Press, 1986.

Beauregard, Mark W. *Railroad Stations of New England Today.* Vol. 1. Flanders, N.J.: Railroad Avenue Enterprises, 1979.

Berg, Walter G. *Buildings and Structures of American Railroads: A Reference Work.* New York: John Wiley & Sons, 1904.

Bohi, Charles. *Canadian National's Western Depots: The Country Stations in Western Canada.* Toronto: Railfare Enterprises, 1977.

Brown, Ron. *The Train Doesn't Stop Here Any More: An Illustrated History of Railway Stations in Canada.* Peterborough, Ontario: Broadview Press, 1991.

Bye, Randolph. *The Vanishing Depot.* Wynewood, Pa.: Livingston Publishing Company, 1973.

Cavalier, Julian. *North American Railroad Stations.* Cranbury, N.J.: A. S. Barnes, 1979.

Coombs, Gary B. *Goleta Depot: The History of a Rural Railroad Station.* Goleta, Calif.: Institute for American Research, 1982.

Culp, Edwin D. *Stations West.* Caldwell, Idaho: Caxton Printers, 1972.

Dixon, Thomas W., Jr. *Chesapeake & Ohio Standard Structures.* Alderson, W.Va.: Chesapeake & Ohio Historical Society, 1991.

Droege, John A. *Passenger Terminals and Trains.* New York: McGraw-Hill, 1916.

Edmonson, Harold A., ed. *Railroad Station Planbook.* Milwaukee: Kalmbach Books, 1977.

Ellington, Frank M. *Santa Fe Depots of the Plains.* Colfax, Iowa: Railroad Car Press, 1984.

Gilbert, John F., ed. *Crossties to the Depot.* Vol. 1, *Virginia Railroad Stations.* Raleigh, N.C.: Crossties Press, 1982.

Grant, H. Roger. *Kansas Depots.* Topeka: Kansas State Historical Society, 1990.

Grant, H. Roger, and Charles W. Bohi. *The Country Railroad Station in America.* Rev. ed. Sioux Falls, S.D.: Center for Western Studies, 1988.

Grow, Lawrence. *Waiting for the 5:05: Terminal, Station and Depot in America.* New York: Main Street/Universe Books, 1977.

Gustafson, Lee, and Phil Serpico. *Santa Fe Coast Lines Depots: Los Angeles Division.* Palmdale, Calif.: Omni Publishers, 1992.

Harwood, Herbert H., Jr. *Philadelphia's Victorian Suburban Stations.* Crete, Nebr.: Railway History Monograph, July 1975.

Historic Railroad Stations: A Selected Inventory Prepared by the National Register of Historic Places. Washington, D.C.: Office of Archeology and Historic Preservation, National Park Service, 1974.

Jones, Wilson E., ed. *The Next Station Will Be . . . An Album of Photographs of Railroad Depots in 1910.* 10 vols. Livingston, N.J.: Railroadians of America, 1973–1989.

Lewis, Edward A. *New England Country Depots.* Arcade, N.Y.: Baggage Car, 1973.

———. *Reading's Victorian Stations.* Strasburg, Pa.: Baggage Car, 1976.

Lord, Robert F. *Downeast Depots: Maine Railroad Stations in the Steam Era.* Collinsville, Conn.: privately printed, 1986.

Martin, J. Edward. *Railway Stations of Western Canada.* White Rock, B.C.: Studio E, 1980.

Orrock, J. W. *Railroad Structures and Estimates.* New York: John Wiley & Sons, 1918.

Parker, Francis H. *Indiana Railroad Depots: A Threatened Heritage.* Muncie, Ind.: Ball State University Department of Urban Planning, 1989.

Parkinson, Richard Marion. *Light Railway Construction.* London: Longmans, Green, 1902.

Pounds, Robert E. *Santa Fe Depots: The Western Lines.* Dallas: Kachina Press, 1984.

Rapp, William F. *Nebraska C.B.&Q. Depots.* Crete, Nebr.: J-B Publishing Company, 1970.

Reisdorff, James J., and Michael M. Bartels. *Railroad Stations in Nebraska: An Era of Use and Reuse.* David City, Nebr.: South Platte Press, 1982.

Sante Fe: System Standards. Vol. 2. Dallas: Kachina Press, 1978.

Stilgoe, John R. *Metropolitan Corridor: Railroads and the American Scene.* New Haven: Yale University Press, 1983.

Stimson, H. A. *Depot Days.* Lake Worth, Fla.: privately printed, 1972.

Ward, Ralph. *Southern Railway Depots: North Carolina.* Asheboro, N.C.: privately printed, 1991.

Willard, William C. *Maintenance of Way and Structures.* New York: McGraw-Hill, 1915.

Willmot, Elizabeth A. *Meet Me at the Station.* Toronto: Gage Publishing, 1976.

Ziel, Ronald, and Richard Wettereau. *Victorian Railroad Stations of Long Island.* Bridgehampton, N.Y.: Sunshine Special, 1990.

INDEX

THE AMERICAN LAND AND LIFE SERIES